adventures and fun
with a Caribbea

Cookin' & Laughin'

in the Cayman Islands

Suzy Soto

designed & edited
by Leslie Bergstrom

cover photo by David Wolfe

greeting the public as the newly
crowned 'Glamourous Granny', in
Houston, Texas

printed by Toppan Printing Company • Hong Kong

Credits and Thanks

Bob and Sue,
renewal of vows, 1995

This book has been so long in coming, for many reasons. Yet there is a saying that "everything has its own time" and so it has been with this book. There have been many people who have encouraged me and given me faith in myself to finish the task.

The first to mention is my great family! My mom, Jonee Keen's love and belief in me has been never-ending. My husband, Bob Soto, whose only objection was my getting up in the middle of the night and hitting the computer! I think he might have gotten tired of Custard Top Corn Bread and a few other dishes as well. My entire family never said "I am sick of hearing about your cook book, just do it!" although I thought it many times. Many thanks to all of our children and their participation with recipes, photos, and just general encouragement. A special thanks to Leslie Bergstrom, who slaved hours correcting my horrid spelling, did the incredible layout and generally put the book together. My "Family Recipe Section" is dedicated to all of these wonderful people who are the reason my life is worth living...

Great friends have been so encouraging as well. Thanks to Betsy Schrader who did the first editing and spelling corrections. She has contributed some of the poems in the family chapter and we have laughed over plenty of food! At the Tortuga Club, we were lucky to have many illustrious guests, including the author of "The Towering Inferno", who told me to "write on, not to worry about the spelling, that is what editors are for, as creative people usually cannot spell." He was a great encouragement.

Thanks to all of my "special and talented chefs" at the Tortuga Club and Cracked Conch over the years: Cleo Conolly, Vernell Ebanks, Cynthia Senior, Robert Cranston, Audrey Meghie, and Lisa Miller who changed, created, experimented, and cooked some very wonderful food. My English restaurant manager, Thomas Pennington-Lowe, has enabled me to work on this book and other projects by taking care of the business in a most professional manner and with "heart" as if it were his own. And all the others who contributed to the restaurant.

There are others to thank for their encouragement as well: Sara Moulton, the dynamic Executive Chef of Gourmet Magazine. Burt Wolf and his kind words of encouragement. Frank Ambrose, a producer with CNN, who has no idea how his words spurred me on to completion. Frank and Mary Jelinek, a delightful couple, from Media, Pennsylvania, who I came across dining at the Cracked Conch for their radio show on WWDB-FM's "Dining Around"! They too have put out their cook book, "Dining Around" with the best of the recipes they have collected from all over the world. Thanks to all the wonderful customers the old Tortuga Club and now the Cracked Conch By the Sea, whose raves over our food started the whole project. Now you can find out some of the recipes I would not give out! It has been an exciting project and I am grateful for all the encouragement and support!

Suzy and "Barefoot" (George Nowak) receiving awards for contributions to tourism in Cayman.

Foreward

    I recall just about a decade ago Suzy and I were present at some fancy black-tie function (not my kinna gig!) and we were presented with a special award for our contribution to Tourism in the Cayman Islands. After we grinned for the cameras and hugged each other I started thinking..."my gosh, after all these years, I'm still strumming my guitar and singing tropical melodies for the tourists and there's Suzy...after all these years she's still a blond bombshell, cooking up her famous recipes for the tourists." As other patrons sipped fine champagne, I belched and guzzled a few beers while watching Suzy swirl around on the dance floor with her legendary husband Bob Soto. Where does she get the energy???

    "It's been a good run for both of us," I thought to myself... Suzy with her famous husband and Cracked Conch Restaurant and me with a dozen albums to my credit, a house on the beach, a sleek sailin' yacht in the Bahamas and three children. Suzy glides past my table, stops to kiss me on the cheek and I spend the next twenty minutes trying to get rid of her lipstick.

    Well...ten years later into the new millenium, I sit here and write this forward to Suzy's fabulous new book...and guess what? We're still at it. I'm still singing (at a new venue), I have two more children and a lovely third wife and I'm still trying to explain to my second ex-wife about that lipstick. And yes, Suzy is still dancing with Bob. That is when she's not cruisin' on her motorcycle or battling the bureaucrats of our tax-free nation when they attempt to raise taxes.

Suzy's world famous eating establishment is now bigger and better at a new location known as "The Cracked Conch By The Sea". And she has collected even more honors, including winner of America's Glamorous Granny Pageant. Oh my, Suzy a granny? Yap...a herd of 19 grandchildren! Some of them even sing on my children's CD.

Anyway, what can you say about a cookbook, except that these type of publications can be boring. Obviously Suzy realizes that. So, wisely, she has combined her fabulous recipes with a collection of fun stories, photos, drink concoctions and good advice. (note, the Family Recipes section is my favorite part of the book) The end result--a potpouri of delicacies--laughs and well-seasoned information that will make any snobbish chef green with envy.

If you're a seafood lover like I am there is much to be learned in these pages. I can't help but wonder why is Suzy being so generous by giving away some of these GREAT recipes?? Her Cracked Conch recipe for example. This is what has brought her so much fame. And a good old "Fish Rundown"--it's here in these pages. I've often asked some of my local friends for a good rundown recipe and I have yet to get a straight answer until now. Usually they're too inebriated to answer and that's good because a good fish rundown is one of those dishes you cook on a long holiday weekend, in an old metal pot, while picnicking under the shade of a sea-grape tree along some deserted beach. Suzy didn't mention that for a fish rundown you also need a few bottles of rum and a boombox complete with some Barefoot music. This is necessary while you wait out the cooking process.

"Salt Fish and Ackee"...you can't get more traditional Caribbean than that, unless you try the "Peas n' Rice". What the heck...make em' both. Thanks Sue...I never knew you had to cook the rice.

This is a book for everyone. For us ex-patriated or (born n' bred) locals who remember these shores before Burger King or The Holiday Inn, it's full of wonderful memories of the "islands time forgot". For our visitors, it's a must for your souvenir bag. And even if you're not into cooking, you must be into laughing. If you're into none of the above, go climb Mt. Everest on your next vacation and dream about a Suzy's frozen coconut pie.

Enjoy...I guarantee you will.

H.G. Nowak
THE BAREFOOT MAN

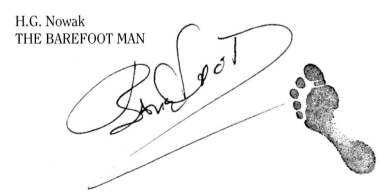

Cookin' and Laughin';
the adventures of a Caribbean family...

Thank you for buying "my cookbook"!

It is my hope that you will find it interesting, entertaining, funny in places, and a bit wacky! Our family left Chicago, Ill., in 1963 in a Buick convertible with 3 adorable young daughters, a live pet turtle, and a Scottie dog named Mac. In 1961, we had vacationed in the little heard-of Cayman Islands and dreamed of sand, sea, and sunshine 365 days per year as a fabulous way of life. It has been an adventure that dreams are made of and unlike the proprietor in Herman Wouk's "Don't Stop the Carnival," who only lasted one year, I have survived almost 45 years of it!!

We built Tortuga Club on the eastern end of Grand Cayman Island during the embargo on Cuba, worrying many of our relatives who thought we had lost all sense. We built 14 rooms, and we ran it for 15 exciting years. We were 32 miles from the main town, George Town; the first 15 miles being chip and spray, then 10 miles of "marl", and the last five miles being only dirt and sand. We had to provide our own electricity, water, fishing, diving, and entertainment! We also had no phone for 5 years. Finally after receiving one, I have never said, "I could rip the phone out!"

Cooking became a challenge as the little island, with a population of 6,000, would sometimes run out of basics like flour, sugar, rice etc. You had to be inventive... ever try Ritz Cracker Pie and pass it off for apple? It works! But I later discovered it is better with a Caribbean squash-type vegetable called cho cho or cristophine.

Somehow my love of cooking grew and developed along with the necessity for working and adapting recipes that I was familiar with, to local style cooking and foreign ingredients. Some of the combinations are great!

The resort became rated as one of the " Top 14 Leading World Resorts". I ran a 98% year-round occupancy and then sold it. Next came the restaurant business, which has been a very exciting and challenging career. During the Tortuga Club years, we had so many requests for recipes, and then for a cookbook, that I began writing and modifying the recipes. During this challenging time, I was also occupied with adding two precious sons and so it has taken nearly 30 years, but here it is!!!

My mother is a fabulous cook, very creative, with a flair for making it right the first time and my children are also good cooks! As a family, we all love to eat. Consequently, several family members have gone on diets, some successful and some not. There are many ideas here for you to substitute ingredients for a lighter dish and I always have an eye out for delicious low-cal dishes. Actually, the healthier preparation is not that much different and many times just as tasty.

Another reason for this "cookbook" is my husband, who thought it unusual that I so enjoyed reading cookbooks at bedtime. This prompted me to add some "other things" for a bit more spice. There is a lot of me in the "Family Recipes", and not what you might expect. There seems to be a lot of advice, conflict, and conversation around lately about having and raising a family, much of it causing confusion. This chapter has been put in to appeal to the good old common sense you were born with, plus the addition of some heartfelt seasonings. I hope this chapter will make you smile.

We have had the honor of having Gourmet Magazine request some of our recipes, and have been recommended by Bon Appetit Magazine. One of our greatest compliments came from Burt Wolf, the famous food editor on Travels and Traditions, his own program, on the Travel Channel and CNN. One of our most exciting guests was Jonathan Winters, his wife Eileen, and their wonderful family. One night he got behind the bar and entertained for almost two hours. It was a night many will remember as this gifted man gave so much pleasure. And we missed it!!!

The restaurant of which we are all so proud is The Cracked Conch By the Sea, in West Bay, Grand Cayman. We are equally proud of our 19 grandchildren from our joined families made up of 8 successful adults plus their wonderful spouses. We keep young by cruisin' on our motorcycles once in a while, boating not often enough, white water rafting, kayaking, among other adventurous pursuits.

So here it is completed and I do hope you will enjoy the "family feeling", little anecdotes and advice and of course some of the recipes!

Love,

Suzy

Enjoy your meals
where'ere you eat
carbohydrates and protein
but less red meat...

I like good food--
eat it every day
I'm certain these recipes
won't be in the weigh!
I watch my fat
keep my protein high
eat lots of fruit
and have a clear eye
(and slim-looking thighs!)
I have a strong desire
to stay in shape
and do not "snack".
Well, maybe a grape...

I hope that you will try this book
you may then know the best way to cook...
with love
with spice
with passion
with zest...

**with an eye to the past
and a taste for the best!**

PROCEDURE FOR SERVING LUNCH

INSIDE

Have tables set up by 12:30 and all set to serve at 1:00. Beverages etc. ready.

Serve ice water as soon as they sit and ask if they would like, ice tea, hot
     tea or coffee. Serve.

Serve lunch, when everyone is finished askx offer them dessert & serve.

OUTSIDE

Wipe off tables, set up knife fork and spoon.

Don't serve ice water, just beverage with lunch.

Serve lime slices in little glass sauce cups. If serving bread or muffins serve
     butter in saucers. Put everything from kitchen in smallest possible dish.

Serve beverages from window seat in bar.

Serve lunch and dessert.

BUFFET

Put everything on serving tables in dining room.

Place mats on all dining room tables. Thatzis Have salt, pepper, & sugar on
     dining room tables, but that is all.
Outside tables just wipe off.

Have everything ready ahead of time and both be in their. Replace food as it
     is getting down to half. Keep cook well informed ahead of time, if it
     looks like something is getting low. Be sure anyone other than guests
     has a chit and pays the bartender.

SERVE FOOD FROM THE LEFT —— REMOVE ——RIGHT

SERVE ALL BEVERAGES FROM THE RIGHT —— REMOVE FROM THE RIGHT.

The one and the only kitchen procedures list that used to
hang on the door of the old Tortuga club.

Contents

a word about ingredients	2
drinks	9
appetizers & treats	17
breads	27
soups	35
salads	45
vegetables and side dishes	51
seafood	65
chicken	85
meat	95
jams and sauces	113
pie	119
special cookies	127
desserts	137
a bit o'candy	153
diets	159
family recipes	169

A word about ingredients...

West Indian cooking is a fantastic blend of many different cultures, indicative of all the islands and their history. Some of the most gifted cooking in the world comes from this region.

My suggestions are basic, some forced by necessity, and after running a tiny hotel on one end of an island that often ran out of flour, "creativity was definitely the mother of invention!"

You will find my suggestions tend to be on the simple or easier side; life is too short and who wants to waste it straining and draining the seeds, pulp, and bulk that it seems all diets are lacking? Whoever prefers strained, plain jelly instead of a rich thick jam will not want this book!

Fresh herbs add that extra gourmet touch to many dishes. I like to grow basil, tomatoes, aloe and rosemary outside my front door. They are very easy and thrive indoors or out. Basil is super for your soups and bean dishes. Dressings with oil and vinegar are so good with fresh herbs; different ones all giving a new slant on the basic flavor. There are so many new oils; i.e. olive oil with garlic, and it's the same with vinegars. Experiment.

Some interesting ingredients:

The **"Scotch Bonnet pepper"**... She is small and each one has a "squdgy" different shape. Her colors are varied: yellow, greenish, orange and all put together. Watch out-- She's potent... my first experience was disastrous! I had promised Lingard, our yard man, that I would buy some papayas he had for sale. There were no guests in the hotel but I assumed a few papayas would be good for the family. The next day I found 75 lbs of green papaya awaiting me. Keeping a promise is important so I paid him, thinking to myself, "what on earth am I going to do with 75 lbs of green papaya?" Well... chutney was the answer. I got a basic recipe and proceeded to use Scotch Bonnet pepper for the heat in my "papaya chutney".

I was in the hotel kitchen busily flicking out the seeds in the pepper with my fingernails. My dear friend Cleo came in and astounded, said, "Miss Sue, you're gon ta burn yur fingers off!" I replied, "never mind, it 's too much trouble to flick them out with utensils". An hour later, my hands were on fire..... there was no relief until I thrust them into a bucket of sea water and soaked them there. Thus my introduction to the local pepper! Cleo and I are still close friends and we worked together creating wonderful food for 16 years.

The Scotch Bonnet is a very important ingredient in our cooking. Actually, we make a garnish which is used as a relish on cooked foods, as a marinade on precooked meats and fish, and as a secret ingredient in all kinds of recipes one would never suspect. To make the pickled peppers you take about 2 doz. of the Scotch Bonnets, remove the stems, forget removing the seeds, as they too have flavor and value, put them in the blender with red wine vinegar or any vinegar, or save your dill pickle juice and use that instead. Blend, adding other marinating ingredients, and onion, garlic, etc. Once you have this in your fridge, you will have plenty of use for it. Salt can be cut down by using other seasonings instead, and the pickled Scotch Bonnet is a good place to start. Remember to wear rubber gloves, or use utensils, and do not touch your face or eyes while dealing with these Caribbean peppers or chilis. The volatile oils can and will burn your skin! You will have other hot peppers in your area and you may use those in substitute for the Scotch Bonnet.The old standby tabasco sauce is also good.

Pickapeppa is a seasoning that, once used, is hard to live without. It is made in Jamaica and I remember a time when the factory closed down with the rumor that they would never open again. I rushed out and bought all I could find. Then there was speculation about the recipe being a "family secret" and they would not give it to anyone else to produce. Whatever happened, it did close down for a short time, but is still available and I am hopeful it always will be. It is made with West Indian spices including tamarind and papaya, which is such a good tenderizer. Anyway, this is an ingredient that I use frequently and panic if I have less than 3 bottles on my seasoning shelf. It is great for marinating meats, fish, and adds just the right touch to many soups, stews, etc. It can be added to cream cheese, making it a delicious dip or cracker spread. It certainly replaces A-1 and Worcestershire sauce in my kitchen. It just has that extra tang. In any of the recipes, you may substitute worcestershire sauce for the Pickapeppa sauce.

Aloe is a miracle medicinal plant. It is used for a wide variety of things. The plant itself is very pretty with green narrow stalks that grow out of the ground and spread out like fingers and everyone in the tropics should have one in their yard. My front door is graced with some on either side so I do not have to go far for a cure for a cut, sunburn, or lotion for my face and body. It is also good to make a drink out of and many Islanders proclaim its healing properties for over-weight, diabetes control, and general overall health. I knew a very special lady in the Brac, Miss Zene whose health was failing. A lady working with her fixed a drink with about 1/2 blender full of cranberry juice, apple juice, two inches of the aloe, and any fresh fruits like a banana, grapes, apple, mango, and papaya that are around. Whir this up in the blender and drink 8 oz per day. Miss Zene's health so improved, her weight dropped, her swelling went away, and there was a general improvement. It is a delicious pick- me-up and I do believe it has healing benefits for "what ere ails ye"! I had the flu the other day and it knocked it out in 2 days! I also have a contractor friend who had a serious bleeding ulcer. His doctor recommended that he drink aloe every day. He did so for one month and when he went back the ulcer was healed, and there was not even a sign of a scar where the ulcer had been. I must stop, for these stories could fill a book!!

When cutting the aloe you must be careful that the sticky juice does not get on your clothes, as it does stain. Also when adding it to a drink, you do not need to peel off the skin entirely. I cut off the two sides that have prickles on them and put the rest in the blender. It works out just fine.

Crushed garlic and lime juice are wonderful for marinating meats, fish and poultry before cooking. A definite must: season yucca (cassava) with garlic and lime after cooking then add some butter and salt...

Coconut milk; Finding a fit coconut is fairly easy: it will be brown, but still have some water inside that you can hear when it's shaken. You must then find someone to break it open or do it yourself which could be dangerous if you are not adept at handling a machete. Next, pull away the husk to reveal the nut. Then puncture a hole through the three eyes at the end of the nut and drain out the wonderful coconut water into a cup to drink as this is very nourishing and supposedly good for kidney and bladder problems. Then you crack the nut and dig the pieces of hard coconut out of the nutshell. You can also put the nut in the oven at 350° for a short time and it is supposed to open up itself, as the outside shrinks and makes it easier to separate the coconut. I find it all hard work and relegate that to the men in the family. It has become a good business for several companies who now sell the plain tinned coconut milk! It does add flavor and the right touch, but again the health experts say that coconut oil is bad for you. However, the older folk in the islands used it daily and many of them are still living to tell you so! If you substitute canned coconut milk, make sure you use the non-sweetened variety, as there are other types used in making Pina Coladas, which are thicker and sweetened.

How to make coconut milk:

Put the pieces of coconut in the blender with very hot water and blend on high, getting the milk out of the coconut trash. Pour into a bowl and squeeze the coconut to get the liquid out. Repeat until the coconut has been thoroughly squeezed. Put through a strainer into another bowl, pressing and squeezing the rest of the milk out. Throw away the trash, and use your coconut milk.

Some people call coconut water coconut milk. The two are not the same. The water is what is drained from the coconut and the milk is the liquid "essence" of the coconut meat. Also if you pick the coconut when it is still a bit green, save the water, and get a spoon and scrape out the "coconut jelly", before it has hardened. This is a real treat!

Ackee is the oblong fruit of an ackee tree. The scarlet pod encloses cream colored flesh resembling scrambled eggs, tasting a bit nutty, but smooth. It is normally served with codfish and is considered Caribbean soul food. If eaten before the pod ripens and breaks open it can be poisonous. Canned ackee is very delicious seasoned and slightly cooked with bacon, herbs like garlic and parsley, and makes an interesting spread for crackers.

Tamarinds are brown brittle pods in a large finger shape with sticky pulp inside around the seeds. They sort of resemble enlarged rounded pea pods, with individual peas inside. Tamarinds are also known as Indian Dates and come from a lovely tree with wispy fern-like leaves. A paste is made from the extracted seeds which tastes a little like dried sour-sweet apricot. About 1 C. pulp mixed with 3/4 C. brown sugar works as a base for cool drinks, mixed with water or plain soda. The easiest way is to wash and shell the tamarind, cover them with water overnight, then simmer gently until the seeds fall from the fruit. If you are making jam or "tamarind butter" use 2 C. pulp to 1 C. brown sugar, boil until thick, stirring constantly. Put in the fridge in a tightly covered jar. If preserving, to keep unrefrigerated, follow normal sterile canning procedures. In the past, this fruit was also used medicinally; the pulp as a laxative, the seeds an astringent, and the leaves for curries and yellow and red dyes. The tree has a heavy hard wood, which was also used in carving.

Coconut Rum is rum with coconut flavoring added to it. I use this in many recipes and it is not quite detectable, but it is delectable! I always use a small amount in making a boxed chocolate cake or brownie mix and just gives that special oomph!

Naseberry or Sapodilla is near to pear consistency with a tannish brown skin with little hairs. Very delicious with its own unique flavor.

Eggfruit has a delightful taste with the reverse color of an egg; the center white and the outside yellow. There was a tree outside Dr. McGregor's and it was always a treat to pick and eat the eggfruit!

Some of the others are **star apple, sweetsop, and soursop.** They all have distinctive fruity flavors and are delicious when seeds are picked out and put in a blender with a bit of liquid to make a fruit drink.

Beautiful Breadfruit!

This has a romantic history, having been transported to the Caribbean by the famous ship "The Bounty", the star of the classic movie "Mutiny on the Bounty"!

This is indeed a beautiful starch that grows in abundance on a lovely tree. It is big like a coconut, but green, with a bumpy surface, and it may weigh up to 10 lbs. Its texture resembles a potato, sort of, and any recipes with potatoes can be converted for use with the breadfruit. Here are a few I wish to give you.

Preparing a breadfruit Peel the green skin off and slice into quarters, down from the stem area. Cut out the pithy middle part down to the solid meat, sort of like a melon. In the old days, they just washed the breadfruit and roasted it whole over hot coals. They would remove the pithy part and stuff the center with a meat loaf type mixture and put it back and roast it longer until done over the hot coals. You can use the oven and do it the same way.

Some delicious ways of preparing breadfruit are:
- Breadfruit salad, prepared in the many ways of potato salad
- Just plain boiled and served with butter, salt and pepper
- Creamed breadfruit
- Scalloped breadfruit
- Fried breadfruit chips (be sure to slice thin, thin, and salt as soon as they are drained on paper toweling)
- Mashed breadfruit (this one can get gluey...I don't use it)
- Use the breadfruit in any of your soups, stews, etc. as you would potato.
These are a few suggestions, it is a real romantic treat this breadfruit, so get some and use your imagination.....

When you find a good breadfruit, you may not be able to eat all of it at once, as it is quite large. What you can do is parboil it and freeze it. Prepare as above and just do not leave in the boiling water as long as the one you are cooking to eat right away. Remove, place in a baggie, seal tightly, and freeze. To serve, do not defrost, but remove from the freezer, place in boiling water, and cook until soft. I like mine soft, my husband prefers it a bit firmer, so boil to your liking.

Cassava This is a wonderful root that is grown throuout the West Indies. Many things are made of it as it is a starch that is adaptable to a variety of preparations. Bread, cakes, and mainly as a starch instead of potatoes or rice. Cornstarch is made from cassava

5

so it can boil down and make its own sauce by adding butter, garlic, and lime juice. It also can be sliced, parboiled, and fried.This is delicious instead of french fried potatoes.

Banana, Plantain, Bottlers, and Apple Bananas

When I first ventured into the Caribbean, I didn't know there was a host of different bananas and that two of them are not edible uncooked! Bottlers and plantains must be cooked or they cause one big bellyache! The banana plant is a giant herb, producing one of the most beautiful and nutritious fruits. When it puts out one "hand" of bananas, there are new shoots that come up around it. After the "hand" has ripened and been cut off, the tree should be chopped down and the new shoots will grow up in the same area.

The normal 'Chiquita' banana is eaten raw or cooked and one of its favorite uses is in Banana Bread. The "apple banana" is of the same family, but with a slightly tart, apple flavor. It is half the length of the normal banana, the skin much thinner like tissue paper, and it must be ripe to eat. It is perfect when the skin begins to fall off and there are black spots on the skin. Delicious! The plantain is larger than the eating bananas, with thicker skin, and can be prepared while the skin is green, yellow, or ripe (almost black). I prefer my fried plantain ripe and black and when they are cut diagonally and fried, they are soft and tender, sweet and delicious. I do not like them fried yellow--then they are stiff and dry. The plantain may be boiled green and served with meat or fish, used as the starch or "bread kind" in Fish Rundown, and in West Indian recipes. It is definitely not edible without cooking and when cooked green it is starchy, not sweet. The botanical name is "musa paradisiaca."

Helpful cooking hints:

1. Boil plantains peeled or unpeeled, whole or sliced, green or yellow. Peel green ones under running water to avoid staining hands and clothes. Cook for 30 min. Serve plain as a vegetable with margarine, salt and pepper.

2. Cut green plantain thin, and fry plantain chips in hot oil, draining on paper towels, salt immediately. Be careful not to burn. These are delicious!

3. Fry ripe plantains, as described above, sliced and fried over low heat, until plantain is soft and slightly brown on each side. Drain on paper towel, salt and serve.

4. Take ripe plantain (black), place on foil, slit top of plantain open and squeeze ends toward center making opening pocket, pour in some rum or coconut rum, put on a little brown sugar, and bake in foil for about 20 min. Take out and serve in foil, with whipped cream or Cool Whip on top. You can scoop out the hot plantain and serve in dessert dishes if you prefer. This works for all the bananas...

5. These also make good dumplings: grate green plantain and mix with an equal amount of flour & a pinch of salt and mix until you can form into finger-like shapes, adding them to soups and stews. You can also make it with the soft ripe plantain or bottler, where grating would not be necessary. Just mash it and add flour until the right consistency to roll into shapes, again adding to your soups and stews.

The bottler is of the same family as the plantain, its size is shorter and stubbier, but all the above applies to the bottler.

Papayas

Papayas are reputed to be the key to longevity! The papain which is from the papaya, is used in meat tenderizers. Some women use it mixed with yogurt and put it on their faces for a quick lift. However, the unripened fruit and milk can cause allergic reactions from the enzyme in the skin and the unripened flesh. When freshly picked, the first "white milk" from the papaya can stain clothes. This is why sometimes you'll see a papaya in a home, with slits cut down the skin and set aside to drain, letting the milk drain out. Some people never bother doing this, but they cut the fruit when ripe and are careful about handling, washing up after preparation is completed.

More information is contained in my Papaya Chutney recipe. I have also used the green papaya as a vegetable, boiled or steamed and served with salt, pepper and butter. I have even added a cheese sauce over the cooked papaya chunks, then baked it and it was delicious.

Mangoes

This is one of my very favorite fruits! Try my mango jam recipe; it's great! Again, take care of the fluid secreted beneath the skin, it can cause allergic reactions. There are many different types of mangoes: My choice is a must...mangoes without strings.... they are a pain to me and I do not eat them. The strings get in my teeth and get stuck and I look like a 'Monster from the Deep,' with fruit fibre strings hanging out of the tight divisions

between every tooth...The flavor of these can still be great and they can be cooked and strained for jams, sherbet etc.

Some of the best mangoes to look for are: Haden, Peppermint, St. Julie, and local ones. To peel a mango, cut the end from the stem and peel down. The very best way is to get in the sea first, bite off the end and peel with your teeth!

Nutrition Action magazine states that, "papaya is, overall, the best fruit in the world, with mangoes second." What more can you ask for??

Suzy, Burt Wolf, CNN food writer, and his son outside the Cracked Conch. It great to count Burt as a fan and a friend!

Here is a special poem that was recited by Phoebe Spence of East End It's in a recording, which to me is priceless....

The author is unknown, but this is quite old and has been around Cayman for years. I also came across it among the Amish in Wisconsin....

Young at Heart

How do I know my youth has been spent
Because my get up and go, got up and went;
But in spite of all that, I'm able to grin
When I think where my get up and go has been.

Old age is golden, I've heard it said
But sometime I wonder as I go to bed
My ears in a drawer, my teeth in a cup,
My eyes on the table until I wake up.

When I was young my slippers were red
I could kick my heels right over my head
When I grew older my slippers were blue
But I could still dance the whole night through.

Now I am old my slippers are black
I walk to the corner and puff my way back,
The reason I know my youth is spent
My get up and go has got up and went.

I get up each morning and dust off my wits
Pick up the paper and read the "obits"
If my name is missing, I know I'm not dead
So I eat a good breakfast and go back to bed!

Tropical Libations

Lindy serves up one of our famous tropical drinks at the Cracked Conch bar.

Tolmacks' Margarita

This is a recipe from a very dear friend of ours, a well known neurosurgeon, and second to none as a chef!! It is always a treat to have him cookin'! Anyway, he makes a mean margarita and here is the recipe...It works for 4 to 6 people, depending on the size of the glasses. Cut in half for 2 people. Or maybe not!!

First, make sure to get the large round margarita glasses with stems... Never tastes right if it is not in a proper glass. Rub the rim with a fresh lime and roll in salt that you've poured on a plate, to have the glass properly prepared...

```
2   6 oz cans frozen limeade
12 oz Cuervo Gold Tequila
2/3 C. Triple Sec
4 C. ice
```

Mix in two sections, putting half the ingredients into blender and blending on high slowly adding remaining 2 C. ice. Pour into glasses. Mix second batch and serve. You may want a bit more ice, but they are really good just like this. I found it to be good for 4 servings with a half of a glass as a dividend; all you really need for a good evening!!!

"Caymanian Holiday"

In the "old" days, the drink with the biggest kick was very popular. Now in this time of more sensible and moderate drinking habits, this would be considered a very potent, but delicious drink! The limit should be one...two at the most...In the past, three was a record to walk away from and that was held by only one very strong man!

1 jigger med. rum
1 jigger light rum (Appleton, Bacardi not dark or white lightning)
1 jigger brandy
1/3 jigger orange Curacao
2 jiggers pineapple
1 jigger lime juice
1 jigger fruit syrup

Serve over chopped up ice cubes.. Serve in a Hurricane glass, or closest thing you can find to it, and watch out for the hurricane!

Sorrel

A tropical Caribbean Christmas drink made from a plant called Sorrel. Sorrel is in the Hibiscus family (Hibiscus sabdariffa) and the only one that bears fruit. It is a beautiful red color and makes a festive drink. Buy the red "calyx petals" which have been removed from the pods and the stems. Put into your pot and cover with water, and bring to a boil, adding your spices. The Island way is to add fresh ginger, about 1 inch to 2 lbs. sorrell and about 2 C. brown sugar, and let it steep overnight. In the morning strain it and add red wine or rum, either one helps it keep longer. I do not like ginger, so I prefer eliminating the ginger, adding 1 stick cinnamon or 1/2 tsp.powdered cinnamon, 2 C brown sugar and the juice of 1 lime. Some people do not like sorrel and do not realize it is due to the strong ginger flavor. Refrigerate. When serving you may add the rum or wine, whichever your 'customers' prefer!! This makes about 1/2 gal.

Pisco Sour

A Peruvian propaganda drink!! Peru sells so much Pisco Sour liquor to tourists I'm sure it helps with the national debt! Funny, when we got home it seemed like we only made a few drinks. I am not sure what happened to the Pisco Sour Liquor??? It just went so fast... Whatever, it is a fun drink for a South American Party! Watch out though, very sneaky...

    2 jiggers Pisco Sour liquor
    1/2 jigger liq. bar syrup
    1/2 egg white (powdered egg white is easier)
    1/2 lime
    1 drop Angostura Bitters
    Crushed ice

Whirl quickly in blender and serve in small old fashioned glasses.

What's Cuba's national drink?...

Cuba Libre?... Nooooo ..."Mojitos"!

Our Cuban friend, Virginia Hernandez, served these to us in Bimini in the sea, starting at 10 A.M. I told my husband I was definitely not an A team drinking member and would be dead on arrival to anywhere if I started my day with those... I've also had them in Ernest Hemingway's favorite bar in Havana, La Bodeguita Del Medio, where they were 'invented' and we watched the authentic preparation! When you finish drinking, you can write your name on the wall. These are for the strong at heart and everything else!!

    1 small sprig fresh mint leaves per drink
    2 jiggers white rum (again not white lightning)
    2 tsp. sugar or to taste; some like it sweeter
    Crushed ice
    1 tsp. lime juice
    club soda to fill

In a tall, slim glass, put mint leaves in and crush down with a spoon, add rest of ingredients, filling with club soda last.Stir together. They made up pitchers, crushing the mint leaves in the bottom and pouring everything on top and stirring.

Cuba Libre

Coke, a splash of rum, lime... Great, refreshing and make it your style according to strength.. A slice of lime or sprig of mint is a nice touch. I like to use a good smooth tasting coconut rum instead of regular rum, and diet Pepsi. It makes me think I'm being 'weight conscious'.

Mudslide

This is just basically a dessert... There are all types of recipes. You will want to modify according to your caloric intake!

1 jigger of Kahlua,
1 jigger of Tia Maria,
1 jigger of vodka
1 Bailey's Irish Cream
1/2 jigger Frangelico,
2 scoops of chocolate chip ice cream....

Put into the blender and serve. Fill straw with kahlua and dust with chocolate powder. Serves two. Yum!

Pina Colada

This is the delicious drink of the tropics!

2 jiggers of pineapple juice,
2 jiggers of coconut milk
2 jiggers of rum (use a good light rum or coconut rum)

Put into the blender with a 1/2 C crushed ice and blend until smooth. Now for a real treat, put in a shot of Bailey's Irish Cream, for a Bailey's Pina Colada; a popular drink at Cracked Conch. For the coconut milk use Coco Lopez, the sweetened canned coconut milk. Some people use the cheap 150 proof "white lightning" that tastes like some kind of fuel...If you're going to all this trouble, use the good stuff! Try the coconut rum, which is what I use. Serves 1.

Conched Out Special

Many of our customers like this drink--it's a house favorite!!

    1 jigger dark rum
    1 jigger light rum
    1 jigger brandy
    1 jigger cointreau
    3 jiggers pineapple juice
    3 jiggers coconut milk (Coco Lopez)
    splash of lime

Shake heartily and serve in a tall glass on the rocks. Serves two.

Having a nice chat in The Old Tortuga Club bar.

The 'Suzy' Special

    This was the 'Welcome Drink' served at the old original Tortuga Club from opening in 1963 and for the next 15 years. Every guest was greeted with one of these with a Hibiscus placed on the side. I also used bamboo for the glasses. I would find the bamboo poles on the beach, cut, clean, and varnish, then serve the drinks in them. It was a great smooth drink, not overpowering, and not that yucky sweet rosy rum punch everyone serves, a bit on the tart but refreshing side.

    THE 'SUZY SOTO SPECIAL':
1.5 oz gold rum
1.5 oz light rum
2 oz Pineapple Juice
2 oz ginger ale
1 oz lime Juice

The 'Bob Soto' Special

These are a favorite at our restaurant and among several family members, who request to remain anonymous. These two variations on the same basic drink are refreshing, fruity and a little different. Very good teamed with a sunset and a bunch of good friends and family!

    1.5 oz coconut rum
    1.5 oz light rum
    2 oz pineapple juice
    2 oz ginger ale
    1 oz lime juice

Uncle Walter's Milk Punch.. or "The-Morning-After-Saver!"

Uncle Walter doing what he did best.

It works, it's good..its smooth....

My Uncle Walter would come down to the island and he and I entertained the guests by putting on grass skirts and doing the Hula Hula! He was my idol-- he looked like Errol Flynn, with a deep golden tan, white hair and a mustache. All the women fell for him, but it was my Aunt May who had him!!!

This was a favorite at Tortuga Club, especially after one of our dance nights.
1 1/2 tsp sugar
a bit of shaved lime peel, (zest) or a <u>touch</u> of lime juice
3 shots milk or 2% milk
1 shot light rum
Put in blender and serve in tall frosty glasses
Sprinkle of nutmeg on top.   MMMmmmmmm............

'Troubling Trouble'

We poor humans tend to borrow
Trouble that may be due tomorrow,
But when tomorrow becomes today
And imagined trouble fades away,
We never pause to wonder why,
Nor appreciate its passing by,
Instantly we start to borrow
Trouble that may be due tomorrow.

a few sayings about town...

The person who rows the boat generally doesn't have time to rock it.

Yelling at your kids to get them to obey makes as
much sense as driving your car by honking the horn.

If your foot slips, you may recover your balance.
If your tongue slips, you cannot recall your words.

You can't keep trouble from coming,
but you needn't find it a chair to sit on.

Those who do not cross rivers until they get there, have few to cross.

The right temperature of home is maintained by warm hearts,
not hot heads.

There are 2 kinds of fishermen, Those who insist they fish for sport,
and those who catch something.

A woman I greatly admired, found this on a tombstone in Scotland;
"Where ere you go, where ere you be,
Always let the wind blow free,
Cause holding a "fart" was the death of me!!"

Guess who!
Serving up treats at the
Lighthouse school annual
Christmas party.

thoroughly appetizing appetizers & treats

Barrie's Salsa

My dear daughter Barrie and her family eat healthy. She gave me this recipe to try to wean me away from my more "splurgy" dips! Mix together and chill before serving. Serve with tacos or crisps of some sort.. Delicious.

2 C diced fresh plum tomatoes
1 1/2 C diced red bell peppers
1 1/2 C chopped onion
2 large jalapeno peppers seeded and diced
1 14.5 oz can plum tomatoes not drained, remove tomatoes and chop
6 garlic cloves minced
1/4 C chopped cilantro
1/4 C. chopped fresh parsley
1/4 C. lime juice
2 Tbs. chopped fresh oregano
1 Tbs balsamic vinegar
1 tsp. ground cumin
1/4 tsp. salt
1/4 tsp pepper
1 5.5 oz can V8 juice

Guacamole

2 ripe avocados
2 Tbs lime juice
2 Tbs chopped onion
1 clove garlic
1 Tbs Pickapeppa
3 Tbs mayonnaise (low fat OK)
1 tomato peeled and finely chopped
salt & pepper to taste
2 chopped chili peppers, Scotch Bonnet sauce, tabasco, etc.

Chop avocados, mash with lime juice, add rest of ingredients, and mix well. No need to put into blender, unless you want it smooth, but guacamole should have a rough texture. Ingredients can be varied without too much sacrifice so be creative. Serve with tacos.... Delish!

Caviar Pie

This is very easy and a big family favorite!!

2 to 3 1/2 oz jar black lumpfish caviar or amount determined by shape/decorating.
2 to 3 1/2 oz jar red lumpfish caviar.
1 Tbs. Pickapeppa sauce
1/2 tsp. Tabasco
1/4 tsp. crushed garlic or garlic salt
1/2 C. finely chopped scallion or onion.
1 C. finely chopped parsley
16 oz cream cheese

Mix all above ingredients except for caviar. Soften cream cheese, adding ingredients. Place into mold or mold with hands into desired shape. You may need to add a touch of milk, to make the cream cheese workable. You may use low fat cream cheese but the no fat just doesn't work. The best results come with the solid brick cream cheese. The low fat tends to get runny. Cover with caviar in patterns or shape as a fish using black olive in middle for the eye ball, pimento strips for mouth, etc. Often I have prepared it for a wedding in the shape of a heart, using one color for the names of the couple, and the other color around the name. Once I even made it for a baby shower in the shape of a baby!! Cover the entire shape with the caviar. Outlining may be done with white cream cheese pushed through a cake decorator. Make the day or two before and refrigerate. The lumpfish caviar may have a strong fishy taste and the dye may run when placed on the form. I like to put it in a strainer, gently wash it with water and put into paper towel to dry before placing on the shape. This gives a much better look. I have also been using the salmon caviar which is a little more expensive but has a better taste.

Sons Jim, Randy and Kris on yet another adventure. Wherever we go, we always enjoy our food!!

Conch Fritters

We have never given this recipe out, so we would appreciate it if you would keep it for yourself and it is not to be reprinted in any other cook-book. Thank you!

4 lbs. conch
2 green peppers
1/2 head celery
2 onions
6 eggs
1 1/2 t. salt
1 1/2 t ground thyme
1 1/2 black pepper
3 T. baking powder
4 cups all purpose flour

Put first 4 ingredients into a food grinder and drop by the teaspoonful into hot oil. Fry until lightly browned, serve with tartar sauce.

Dream Dip

This stuff, ominously called 'Gook', sounds so dreadful! However, it is an old family recipe from Oshkosh, Wisconsin made famous by a great lady and cook; Mimi Gibson. I guarantee this to be absolutely delicious and truly a "dream dip" in preparation as well as taste!

20 oz. soft cream cheese
1 Tube of anchovy paste
1/4 pint whipping cream
4 tsp. crushed parsley flakes

Mix together and serve.....It can be made on the lighter side by using light cream cheese and 1/2 fat free half and half. Ruffles chips and pretzel sticks are great to dip with!!

Fruited Cheese Ball

An appetizer to do a couple of days before a party.

2 8 oz pkg cream cheese
4 tsp. chopped dates
2 tsp. orange or mango Tang
4 tsp. chopped nuts (walnuts)

Combine all ingredients, form into 2 balls and roll in more chopped nuts until covered. Wrap in saran wrap and refrigerate. Easy, easy!!

Hot Crab Dip

My mom was a wonderful cook. She entertained a lot and this was a favorite of her guests.

1 lb. Velveeta cheese,
2 glasses Old English sharp American cheese.
4 tsp. cream
2 C. fresh mushrooms, chopped
2 C. pitted ripe olives, sliced thin,
2 C. crab meat, cleaned and drained.
1/2 C. sherry
1 Tbs Pickapeppa sauce or Worcestershire sauce

In a double boiler melt 1 lb. Velveeta and sharp American cheese. Slowly add cream, mushrooms, olives, and crabmeat along with one tablespoon Pickapeppa sauce, and a touch of hot pepper. Immediately before serving add 1/2 C. sherry and stir; Should be the consistency of thick heavy cream. Serve warm with Ritz crackers. Place this in a chafing dish to keep warm. Do not overheat or it will ruin the cheeses.

Son Kris belting it out...
We're a real family of singers--so much so that we have our own professional karaoke setup at right at home!

We start 'em early around here!

Leslie's Shrimp Dip

Got this from my daughter in law, Leslie Bergstrom, who claims she doesn't know how to cook... Leave it to someone like this to make it simple!

1 can Campbell's Cream of Shrimp soup
1 pkg cream cheese
1 stick of butter
1 4 1/2 oz drained tin baby shrimp
Pinch of tarragon
Pepper
sprinkle of fresh chives

Let cream cheese get soft, or microwave slightly until soft. Mix in the rest. Chill and serve with crackers. We are hooked on Wheatsworth crackers and the 7 grain octagonal crackers, which are great for this dip.

Rene's Crackers

These are so flavorful, my stepson made them for us when we were sailing, they keep in the refrigerator in a tightly sealed baggie and make a great snack instead of candy, as well as delicious with drinks!!

1 bag regular oyster crackers
1 tsp. dried dill weed
1 tsp. Beau Monde (seasoning) (reg. salt is fine)
1 tsp. lemon pepper or lemon peel seasoning
1/4 tsp. cayenne pepper
1 1 oz. pkg dry ranch style dressing (Hidden Valley)
1/2 C. vegetable or corn oil

Place crackers in a large container with a lid, pour oil over crackers & gently shake. Sprinkle dry ingredients and again shake to coat crackers. Remove from container and store in a sealed bag in the refrigerator!!

Rene's Hummus

My stepson is a terrific chef and we always love to talk cooking. He has given me this recipe for the best hummus to serve your dinner guests prior to the main event!

2 cans of regular size chick peas
juice of 4 lemons
2 cloves of garlic
1 C tahini (sesame seed paste)
1/2 tsp. salt

Place all ingredients in a food processor and blend until smooth adding a little cold water to loosen mixture. You may adjust seasoning to taste. Chill and before serving, drizzle with virgin olive oil. Serve with toasted pita bread pieces.

Sausage Balls

This recipe is from E. J. Bodden, a good Southern cook, turned Caymanian!

3-1/2 C. Bisquick
1 lb hot and spicy ground sausage (for mild, or plain, adding hot sauce to taste.)
10 oz grated sharp cheddar cheese.

Combine all ingredients. If dough does not stick together add a small amount of butter. Form 1 " balls, bake on ungreased baking sheet about 10 min. at 400* or until slightly browned. Serve warm. Delicious! May be frozen and baked later! These are always a big hit!!!

Shrimp Mousse

2 tins baby shrimp, soaked in cold water 5 min. drained.
2 tins Shrimp soup
2 8 oz cream cheese, soften in microwave
2 Tbs. Knox gelatin
2 tsp lime juice
sprinkle of dill weed to taste
fresh parsley chopped
1 Tbs Pickapeppa,
Touch of Cayman pepper, tabasco or whatever pepper to taste for some zing.

Soften gelatin in 1/2 C water, add some shrimp soup about 1/2 cup, dissolve gelatin in microwave about 1 min.
Put all ingredients into a bowl mix thoroughly. I use my hand mixer on medium speed, just until blended, because the pieces are good. Add the gelatin. Pour into a glass meat loaf or bread pan. Either spray with Pam or put in saran wrap. Should only take 3 hours to firm in refrigerator. Unmold before serving, decorate with slices of green olives with pimiento, black olives, cucumber, etc. I serve on a leaf of lettuce with a quick cucumber, sour cream, dill weed mix just put on top for a nice flavor. Some like crackers with it.

Stamp n' Go

This is a popular Jamaican dish. It is relatively easy to prepare, but for small groups. It is better than potato chips!

1 C. codfish
1 C. flour
1 tsp. Scotch Bonnet sauce
1 tsp. baking powder
1 Tbs. chopped scallion or onion
salt & pepper to taste
1 egg
3/4 C. milk

Prepare salted codfish the day before serving, by soaking the cod fish and changing water about 4 times to get rid of the salt. Otherwise you may bring to a boil about 3 times, throw off water, boil again, rinsing out the salt well. When salt is gone simmer fish for about 20 min. until fish flakes apart. Drain thoroughly, discard skin and bones. Put in blender with other ingredients and mix. Should be runny, drop by tablespoonsful in hot oil, keeping frying pan on a moderate fire, fry until brown and turn over. Drain on paper towel. Should come out lacy and crispy. Serve with spicy tartar sauce.

Ceviche

Marinating fish in lime juice is actually another form of cooking, to my thinking. If you have some beautiful fresh fish, with tender white flesh, make ceviche or 'escovitch', etc., There are hundreds of ways to do it as there are different ways to spell it, but it's just a good method of preparing raw fish. For 2 cups of cut up fish, use about 1/4 C. lime juice, 1/2 C. chopped mild onion, 1/2 C. green pepper, 1 med. tomato, 1/2 C. chopped celery, mix, cover and leave for at least an hour. We usually cannot wait that long. I gave this to my Dad one day and he had seconds and thirds, until he asked what it was and when someone told him, raw fish, he went white. He was very squeamish about anything, even dove under tables if a parakeet flew around him!

it always helps to laugh at getting older...

I'm Living

Just a line to say I'm living,
That I'm not among the dead;
Though I'm getting more forgetful,
And "more mixed up" in the head.

For sometimes I can't remember
When I stand at the foot of the stair,
If I must go up for something,
Or I've just come down from there.

And, before the fridge so often
My poor mind is filled with doubt'
Have I just put the food away, or
Have I come to take some out?

So, if it's my turn to write you
There's no need in getting sore;
I may think that I have written
 And don't want to be a bore.

So remember, I do love you,
And I wish that you were here;
But now it's nearly mail time,
So I must say, Good bye, dear."

Here I stand beside the mailbox
With a face so very red...
Instead of mailing you my letter
I have opened it instead!!!

loafin' around!
(or breads that rise to the occasion)

Debi's Banana Chocolate Chip Nut Bread

My daughter-in-law Debi is beautiful and skinny as a rake. She is trying to do the rest of us under with her fabulous cooking! This is an incredible breakfast bread, or anytime treat!!

2 C. flour
1Tbs. baking powder
1/2 tsp each salt, nutmeg, cinnamon
1/2C butter
1 C brown sugar
1 beaten egg
3 ripe bananas (overripe is best), mashed to a smooth paste
1/2 C milk
1 tsp vanilla
6 oz milk chocolate chips (optional)
1/2 C crushed walnuts (optional)

Sift together the flour, baking powder, salt, nutmeg, cinnamon and set aside. Cream the butter and sugar until pale & satiny, then add the beaten egg and mashed bananas. Mix well after each addition. Add the flour mixture gradually with the milk and vanilla. Stir in the chocolate chips and nuts. The mixture should be thick but not too stiff. Pour it into a greased loaf or bread pan and bake at 350* for 60 minutes until brown.

Dancing my heart out and giving it all I've got at the Glamorous Granny Pageant in Texas.

Coconut Bread

Always a treat for Sunday breakfast or any time!
12 C. flour
3/4 lb. margarine
2 1/4 C. coconut milk (use 1 can coconut milk)
2 1/2 C. brown sugar
3 eggs
6 C grated coconut
1 Tbs. vanilla
2 Tbs. baking powder
2 1/2 C. raisins
1 1/2 tsp. salt

Stir dry ingredients, add sugar, then beaten eggs with milk, melted short-ening and vanilla. Stir in grated coconut and and floured raisins, blend ingredi-ents and knead slightly on floured board. Shape into loaves and put in greased loaf pan dusted with flour, filling only 2/3 full. Bake in 350* oven about 45 min. until done. Makes 6 loaves. It pays to make a large batch and share with family and friends. Otherwise freeze it for yourself!

Bran Muffins

1 C. all purpose flour or half whole wheat & half white flours
2 C. All Bran
1/2 C. oatmeal
1 1/2 C. water
1 1/2 Tbs. baking powder
1 tsp. vanilla
1 egg
1/4 C. veg. oil or 3 Tbs. margarine or substitute 1/3 C. applesauce
1/2 C. brown sugar
1/2 C. each raisins, coconut and grated carrot
2 Tbs. coconut rum (not necessary but good)

Mix together and pour into greased muffin tins. Bake at 350* about 25 min. Makes a good dozen.

A lovely photo of what family is really about-- Stepcousins Mark and Kristie. The stepcousins are very close in our family and many even live in the same neighborhood!

French Puffs (doughnuts baked)

Every Christmas, we used to serve these for breakfast instead of other food. They sure are sweet to start the festivities on this wonderful day!

    1 2/3 C. butter-flavored or plain Crisco
    2 1/2 C. sugar
    5 eggs.
    Cream together above ingredients

    Mix 7 1/2 C. flour
    2 Tbs. baking powder
    1 Tbs. salt
    1 1/4 tsp. nutmeg
    2 1/2 C. milk

    Mix dry ingredients into creamed ingredients alternately with milk, until smooth, Fill greased muffin cups 2/3 full Bake until golden brown. Immediately and quickly roll in about 3/4 C. melted margarine. Then roll into a mix of 2 1/2 C. sugar and 2 Tsp. cinnamon. When completed roll into the cinnamon and sugar the second time and if there are any left for serving…….. serve warm!! Warm or cold these are incredible!

Johnny Cakes

This one has various names throughout the islands. Johnny cakes, fritters (flitters), and fried dumplings, probably more too! They are simple and just plain addictive!!

2 C. all purpose flour
1 tbs. baking powder
touch of salt
3/4 C water

Water, enough to make it workable, knead about 20 times until dough is right.....let sit about an hour. Roll out about 1/2 inch thick, and cut in triangles. Fry in medium hot oil, do not have too hot or it will burn. If not hot enough it will not cook inside, so test one first. Great with butter and honey...... They puff up and are light inside sometimes a little hollow. Try variations on these by adding cinnamon, raisins, shredded coconut etc. or just plain grated cheese. Can be a very versatile and make a fast additional touch to dinner!

This is from Ester Balderamos, the best johnny cake maker on the island.

Popovers or Yorkshire Pudding

The Yorkshire Pudding is a dish to accompany roast beef... The popovers accompany any meal, so you figure it out!!...Ingredients should be room temperature. It is easy to make and a little different than rolls, muffins, or biscuits. They are hollow in the middle if you have prepared them correctly and fun to put butter and jam into!! Not ,of course, if they are served as Yorkshire pudding; then they go with the meat and gravy on them.

1 C. flour
1/2 tsp. salt
1/2 C. milk
2 eggs
1/2 C. water

Beat the batter well until large bubbles rise to surface, Bake at 400* oven for 20 minutes, turn down to 350* for 10 to 15 min.

31

Sally Lunn

Original Sally Lunn's recipe from the Sally Lunn Inn in London.
4 C. flour
4 Tbs. butter
2 Tbs. sugar
3 eggs
1/2 tsp. salt
1/2 yeast cake

Beat eggs together. Add sugar and yeast dissolved in 1/2 C. lukewarm water. Sift salt with flour and add gradually. Thin with water to consistency of stiff cake batter. Add melted butter last. Put in bowl and let rise 2 to 3 hrs. Pour into greased tube pan or ring mold. Let rise 2 hours. Bake 375* for 50 min. Turn out on platter and serve hot. Leftovers are good toasted.

& now, our version of Sally Lunn...

2 C. flour
1/2 C. brown sugar
3 tsp. baking powder
1/2 tsp. salt
2 beaten eggs
1 C milk
1 stick melted margarine

Beat eggs, sugar, melted margarine, add milk and rest of ingredients. Bake in a square 8 x 8 dish, add crumb topping of 1/3 C brown sugar, 1/3 C. flour, and enough margarine to make crumbly. Sprinkle over top of bread.

This will surely impress your family!!

'Me-an-my-mom', known as Violet or Jonee or Nana-- she is the basis for my knowledge of cooking and love of food.
What a great character she was!

'Me-an-mom's' Sin Buns

These delicious buns are a cross between my, and my mom's, fabulous cinnamon buns and Bimini coconut rolls, plus my own adjustments. If using the Rapid Rise yeast.... make filling first. If regular yeast, you can make filling while waiting for the dough to rise and work on the laundry or whatever... I prefer the slow yeast, makes me feel old fashioned.

Filling:
2 C. freshly grated coconut (do in blender, chopping coconut into small pieces and dropping in a few at a time while running to prevent clogging the machine).
2 C. brown sugar
1 tsp. vanilla
1 Tbs. margarine

Put brown sugar in pot and dissolve sugar stirring constantly. Add butter, vanilla, and about 1 Tbs. water or more, as needed. Melt down and cook stirring a couple of minutes, adding grated coconut. Stir and cook until mixture thickens enough to allow you to spread on the dough.

Dough:
2 Rapid Rise Fleischman's yeast
6 C. all purpose flour
1 1/3 C. water
1/4 C. margarine
2 eggs
1/4 C. brown sugar
1 tsp. salt.
1/4 C. butter- flavored Crisco

Prepare two oblong pans 13" by 9" by spreading margarine all across the bottom, 1/2 C, sugar mixed with 2 tsp. cinnamon, using half to sprinkle across each pan. Use Mom's secret: a little water sprinkled across the whole thing to keep bottoms (which become tops) soft.

Measure flour, sugar, and yeast in bowl, saving about 1/2 C of flour. Add water and melted shortening and butter at about 125* to 130*.

Knead about 4 minutes, working in leftover flour until it is not sticky. Cut in half, let rest about 10 min. Put on floured board and roll out about 13" by 5".

Spread half of filling mixture, sprinkle on about 1/2 C. raisins and, if you wish to sin well, 1/2 chopped nuts! Roll up lengthwise, sealing at the side. Now for some fun.... Get some dental floss and place under the first part of roll 1" from end, bring floss up and cross until it cuts through roll to make a perfect round cut. Put cut sides down into pre prepared pans, cover and set on top of your stove while oven heats up underneath for about 20 min., or until it rise about double. Put in preheated oven at 350* for 20 to 25 min. I turn my pan about halfway through cooking to ensure overall browning. Leave one batch out for eating, the other batch you can freeze in small zip lock bags and take out later, reheating as needed.

Bimini Rolls

Make filling and dough as above, roll out about 13" by 4" and put in coconut filling, cutting at about every 3" ,put in Pam sprayed pan and let rise about 20 min., or until double. Cook about 15 min. at 400*. These are delicious, and sell in Bimini for $1.35 each!!! You could make this a mother/daughter project and sell them to the neighborhood food addicts!

My Mom's Shortcut Cinnamon Buns

Make dough as above or buy frozen dough, roll out 13" by 5" spread on margarine all over (easier to use soft squeeze kind), cinnamon mixture as above and sprinkle with raisins and if you like some coconut flakes. Spray pans and follow above recipe for cutting (you still get to use dental floss), raising and baking.

Cracked Conch manager Thomas Lowe checks the ever popular Sunday 'Local' buffet.
The lobster bisque is always everybody's favorite.

in the soup!

Crab Soup

My Aunt Grace gave me this simple recipe that was served in a fine Maryland crab house restaurant.

1 8oz can of good crab meat
1 can of pea soup
1 can of tomato soup
1 1/2 C of milk or cream, or both according to your fat calories
1 small discrete pinch of curry powder

Put soups into a saucepan, mix and heat well, slowly add milk or cream, stirring to prevent lumps. add crab meat, curry powder, and eat! You can add a dollop of sour cream. Serves 6.

Cheese Bisque

This was one of my old favorites at the original Tortuga Club, everyone loved it, and wanted to know the recipe. I would have them guess and no one was able to detect the carrot in it, which really gives this soup its zing!

1 C. grated carrot
1/3 C. margarine or butter
1/3 C. flour
2 C. 2% or whole milk
1 C. grated cheese
2 C. chicken broth or bouillon

Cook carrot in margarine just until tender. Add flour, stirring until absorbed by the butter, remove from heat, add milk, broth and cook stirring until thick. Put into blender and blend until carrots have almost disappeared, but you can tell they are there. That is the secret for the oomph to this soup. Put back into pot and add grated cheese. Stir until cheese is melted. If prepared ahead and reheated, it may need thinning. Use beer or milk, for thinning only, as desired, but beer can give it a little extra subtle flavor. Salt & pepper to taste. Serves 4.

A few great great friends and family members celebrate the new arrival of the long-awaited new "Captain Charlie", a fully animatronic pirate!!

Iced Coconut Soup

An unusual refreshing cold soup!

1 tin 14 oz. coconut milk (not sweetened as for drinks)
1 C. chicken broth
2 tsp. curry powder
Salt & pepper to taste.

Put ingredients in blender and refrigerate. Can be served with slices of cold honeydew melon. About 4 small servings.

Cold Avocado Soup

1 ripe avocado, peeled and cut up
1 tsp. lime juice
1 tsp. salt
1 tsp. pepper
1 tsp. dill weed
2 garlic buds or 1 tsp. crushed garlic (omit if you hate garlic)
1 C. milk whole milk for richer or 2% or skim, your preference.

Combine all in blender and chill until serving time. A touch of sour cream is nice on top with a sprinkling of chopped parsley, or even paprika for color. A refreshing starter on a hot day. Can be served hot as well.

'Poppy' and his beloved grandkids.

Cream of Broccoli Soup

1 onion, chopped
1 carrot, chopped
2 whole stalks of celery with leaves chopped
2 cloves garlic or 1 tsp. crushed garlic
1 C. chicken stock or bouilon
2 C. cooked broccoli,choppped or uncooked
Salt and pepper to taste
2 chicken bouillon cubes
1 C. milk

Simmer all ingredients, cooking until broccoli is tender. Put in blender and blend until smooth, add milk.

To save time I cook up lots of broccoli the day before with dinner, having enough left over for soup the next day. If you want to thicken you can add cornstartch dissolved in 1/2 C cool water, stirring in until thickened to desired consistency. Of course you can always use real cream and not have to thicken, except in the waistline.

There is a way out, as there is a new version of fat free half and half!

Another version; just simmer the broccoli, add bouillon cubes, simmer until tender, blend, and add some grated sharp cheese for a quick tasty broccoli cheese soup.

Pumpkin Soup

1 small local pumpkin (about 3 lbs.)
Enough water to come up to about 2/3 of your pumpkin chunks
1 Chopped onion,
1 Tbs. liquid or 2 to 3 squares chicken bouillon cubes
1 to 2 buds crushed garlic or tsp. garlic salt
one shake of cinnamon or 1/4 tsp.
1 to 2 tsp. good curry powder
1 Tbs. Pickapeppa sauce
1 tsp. salt
1 tsp. pepper to taste

Again this soup can be so versatile. Cover with water and boil cut up pumpkin until you can easily scrape off the skin, and put back in pot, adding onion, garlic salt, and a slight touch of Pickapeppa sauce. Add rest of ingredients. Depending on desired thickness, you may have to drain some of the water, but reserve some of it in another container, if you need more liquid when blending. Let it cool slightly and put in blender until smooth. Another fun addition at serving time is a touch of sherry and the new Pepperidge Farm Garlic salad croutons. They seem to stay crisp and add to the flavor of the soup. If you want to get fancy you can add a dollop of sour cream or yogurt. Can be served hot or cold. Serves about 8 people. with a little left over to eat cold the next day. Very nourishing and healthy, so I make a lot.

Chuck and Barrie or 'Sea n' B' as they are professionally known, play all over the island and have several CD's of island music. Chuck has played with the Barefoot Man and band for years.

an old Tortuga Club christmas card circa 1971.

Red Conch Chowder

    4 lbs ground conch
    2 onions
    2 sweet peppers
    1 tsp. crushed garlic
    half head celery chopped
    2 lbs carrots
    2 lbs potato
    2 16 oz tins kidney beans (can be omitted but adds body & fiber)
    3 tins of large stewed tomatoes with juice or 1C. tomato paste & 8 C. water.
    salt & pepper to taste.

    Put ingredients through a blender or finely chop them. Add about 8 C. water and tomato paste Bring to a boil, simmer for about an hour. Can be served with a touch of sherry, and a topping of sour cream and chives.

White Conch Chowder

Giving up this recipe is very hard for me!!

6 strips bacon
4 C. ground conch
8 C diced potatoes, not too small
2 C. diced celery
2 C. diced onion
3 Tbs. margarine, or combination of oil & margarine
1 tsp. garlic salt
1 Tbs. parsley flakes or chopped fresh parsley
1 tsp. poultry seasoning
Salt and pepper to taste
Pinch of dill weed
Scant tsp. of paprika
3 C. milk
1 tin Carnation cream (or more milk)
1/3 C. flour (or less corn starch) enough to thicken.

In a cooking pot, cook bacon until <u>crisp,</u> remove. Lightly brown onion & celery in bacon fat. Add rest of ingredients, Put in pot, just cover with water. Bring to a boil and simmer for about 1/2 hour, until potatoes are soft and conch tender. Remove from heat, add 3 C. milk, 1 tin of Carnation cream, (if desired). Thicken with about 1/3 C. flour or substitute less corn starch. Blend thoroughly and put back on fire, stirring constantly to desired thickness, adjusting with milk or cream if necessary. Add crushed bacon pieces. Serve hot.

Be careful not to add anything with lime or vinegar (such as hot pepper sauce) as it may cause it to curdle. (I prefer this with just 2% milk as I can tell the Carnation cream and do not like the taste).... However, some like to use cream without the milk, so in that case increase it to your taste. Keep in fridge, the flavors blend together with time and it is great for the next few days! Makes about 8 to 10 servings.

Vichyssoise
Or Potato Leek Soup

This is a fantastic cold soup, though it can be served hot, and it can have chopped cucumber cooked with the potatoes and leeks and become a delicious cucumber soup. You can also add a tin of shrimp or crab, with a little dill and sherry mixed in and then it's a great seafood bisque. It is so versatile! I have always pronounced it wrong saying "vichyssoise"; the s as silent, when actually the "s" is pronounced, hard like a 'z'.

4 leeks, (chopped, using the bottom white part, and none of the green unless you don't mind having a light green vichyssoise. (One guess what color mine is at home?)
1 C. chopped mild onion
3 Tbs. butter
5 med. peeled Idaho potatoes
4 C. water & 4 chicken bouillon cubes
Pepper to taste
2 C. cream (not canned) or 1% or 2% milk to be added at end.

Sauté vegetables until onion is translucent, add chopped potatoes, add water & bouillon cubes or tinned chicken broth or stock.

Simmer about 20 min. or until done. Let cool until you can handle and put into blender, about 3 separate batches. Fill storage container with base and chill. This can serve about 12 people, after the cream or milk is added. Using a rich cream will take less, the milk is thinner so you do not need so much. If you are in a hurry... use instant mashed potatoes for a serving of about 4 people and mix into the cooked vegetables. I keep base in fridge, adding the milk when I decide to treat myself with an elegant bowl of vichyssoise. I like to top with a little chopped parsley, although the usual is chives. The base is really pretty healthy and low on calories, so you can decide by tasting how many you want to add, even stretching to skim milk just to make it more liquid. The base will be "pasty" without the milk or cream.

Ackee "Vichyssoise"

This is a most delightful combination, so simple yet with a rich full flavor to challenge any vichyssoise with the mere simple preparation of a can opener, blender and a few simple ingredients. Ackees are now available in most grocery stores, the Caribbean section, or gourmet sections. Ackee is the fruit of a tree and has the consistency of scrambled eggs when ripened. It has a most delicious nutty flavor and is used mainly in 'Codfish and Ackee', a mainstay in the Caribbean. However, we stumbled upon this creation and one of our chefs won an award serving it as Cold Ackee Soup. So purchase 2 tins of ackee, open the tin and pour all of it (including liquid) into the blender, blend on high, taste, add some heavy cream, salt, pepper, and if desired 1/2 tin of coconut milk (not sweetened). Blend and taste, if more seasoning is desired you may add a scant undetectable touch of curry powder. Blend well and chill. You may also substitute coconut milk with a touch of sour cream or milk. It makes a smooth soup and is delicious cold or warm, garnished with a dollop of sour cream and /or fresh chopped parsley. My daughter-in-law Leslie garnishes with a little anchovy paste mixed with cream and swirled on top.

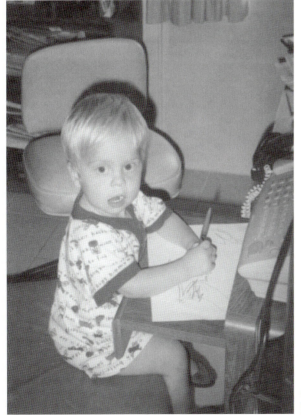

Grandson Jay in my office giving me some help with my cookbook.

A Strange Old Lady...

A weird thing has happened in my life... A strange old lady has moved into my house. I don't know who she is or where she came from. I didn't invite her and I wish she would leave.

She's very clever. She keeps out of sight most of the time, but whenever I pass a mirror, I catch a glimpse of her. Whenever I try to comb my hair or put on makeup, she hogs the whole thing - so that I can't see how nice I look.

I think she has started stealing my money. I go to the ATM, get a hundred dollars and before I know it, it's gone. I can't possibly spend money that fast. I don't know what she spends it on, but a little spent on wrinkle cream would help.

She has a real sweet tooth. I can't seem to keep candy, cookies and ice cream in the house. If she isn't careful, she'll be even fatter than she is.

She gets into my closet when I'm not home and alters my clothes. Nothing fits the same any more.

I'm very neat and organized, but she loves to hide things from me. I'll put something down and the next time I want it, I can't find it to save me. She makes a jumble of my desk and messes up my VCR settings. She gets into my kitchen cabinets and refrigerator, super glues the lids on all the jars and bottles.

Somehow she gets into the car and follows me wherever I go. I see her in store windows when I pass. She puts her favorite things into my cart in the grocery store. In a clothing store, she dons an identical outfit - which looks ridiculous on her. If she'd get out ot the way, maybe I could see how great it looks on me.

She's managed to make stairs steeper, everything is heavier and slower, and she has even used her cunning to affect my vision and hearing.

I don't know what to do to get rid of her. She doesn't even pay rent. If she keeps this up, I swear, I'll put her in a home but first I think I'll check with the IRS and see if I can claim her as a dependent.

Courtesy of Midland Senior Center Newsletter, May 1999

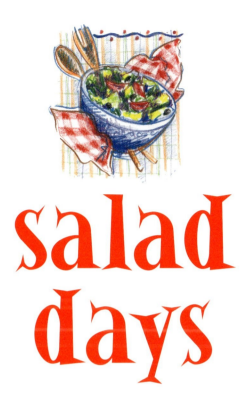

salad days

About salad greens...when preparing salad, carefully wash the lettuce, blot dry with paper towel and place in fridge beforehand to crisp. Only remove when ready to serve, putting dressing on just before serving.

Amazing Banana Peanut Salad

This is controversial... but I love it. Just put down some crisp iceberg lettuce, slice 1/2 banana on top per serving and mix 1/3 C. peanut butter to 2/3 C. light mayonaise and blend well. Put a dollop on top of the banana, they go very nicely together. You may also put a few thinly sliced mild onions on top...

My grandmother ate a sandwich with the above ingredients with lots of onion before bed, and lived to be active until 92 years old! With this, you may just get kids to eat salad!

Elegant Seafood Salad

1 pt. mayonnaise (low fat is fine)
1 1/2 Tbs. lime juice
1 small grated onion
1 1/2 Tbs. of Pickapeppa Sauce
1 small jar of caviar (red salmon caviar looks nice)
1 Tbs. chopped capers
3 English muffins halved and lightly toasted
Fresh sliced tomatoes
3 hard boiled eggs
fried fish cut in small pieces

This recipe is great for using left over fried fish, otherwise fry the fish just for this dish as it is great and different. Mix mayonnaise, lime juice, onion, Pickapeppa, and capers, fold in about 1 cup of cooked fish. Chill in the refrigerator until serving time. When ready to serve, lightly toast muffins, put on plate, add a good slice of tomato, put half of cut hard boiled egg on each tomato slice with flat yoke side next to the tomato and the pointed end on top, cover with fish mixture and put a little caviar on top. Serve. Makes a lovely luncheon dish.

To vary this you may use shrimp pieces instead of the fish, placing a shrimp on top when serving.... serves 3 or 4 people.... It is so good.

46

Caesar Salad

There are hundreds of variations of this famous salad. We serve this at the Cracked Conch By the Sea

1 head romaine lettuce; if not available FORGET Caesar salad!
2 to 4 crushed garlic buds, judged by your garlic tolerance
2 tins anchovies, not drained (I like rolled filets with capers in olive oil)
1/4 C. lime juice
1/4 C. red wine vinegar
1/2 tsp. Cayman hot pepper sauce.
1/2 tsp. garlic salt
1 tsp. black pepper
1 Tbs. Dijon or Grey Poupon mustard (gives added tang)
1 Tbs. Pickapeppa sauce (for flair if desired)
1/2 C. Parmesan cheese (freshly grated, if possible)
1 egg
1 to 1 1/2 C. light virgin olive oil, poured into blender slowly,
     until desired thickness is reached.
1 C. garlic croutons

Put dressing ingredients in blender except for oil. Blend, then slowly add oil. When near desired thickness, add Parmesan cheese in blender as well. This stays nicely in the refrigerator and I like to double the recipe, making enough to last awhile. Use half the dressing to one head of romaine, saving the rest in the refrigerator for another salad. To make a meal out of the salad, the following are some suggested additions:

1/4 C. crumbled Feta cheese or Blue cheese,
a piece of blackened fish, chicken sliced in strips, or salmon
canned or fresh, placed on top of the salad.

Chilled drained canned pink salmon over the top is nice. Use your imagination and eat healthy. This is an ideal way to save calories and serve as a meal in place of a heavy lunch or dinner. Serves two hungry people, or about 6 as a side dish.

Greek Salad

The other night I had a Greek salad at a restaurant and the cucumber chunks were so big I had to slice them to eat them. They were so hard that when I sliced a piece it flew off of the plate. The onions were also sliced so thick, which made it too strong unless cut more. This is unnecessary. So here is my version...

red onion sliced in paper thin rings, (enough for your taste.)
1 tomato, sliced, in chunks
About 1/3 of a cucumber, in thin slices,
About 1/4 of a red or green bell pepper, diced
Pitted black olives or the real Greek olives in oil (add to your taste)
About 1/3 lb feta cheese, crumbled over the salad.
Mix all together with dressing;
Dressing:
1/3 C. lite olive oil
1/2 C. red wine vinegar
Dash of oregano,
Salt & pepper, shake well and pour enough to wet well, just before serving..
Put in refrigerator and marinate up to one day. To me it tastes better.

Authentic Greek salads do not have lettuce. However some people want lettuce with it so you can add 1/3 head of chopped iceberg lettuce or nice leaf lettuce to decorate around plate. Some Greek restaurants also serve a small amount of potato salad, but I do not like that addition.

For a change of pace, top with chilled salmon chunks or tinned salmon... blackened fish, chicken, or whatever. It is good for you, this salad!! Serves about 2 people.

Our beloved 'Aunt Jeanne'-- a gourmet cook to beat the band, at a family Christmas gathering.

Red Roquefort Dressing #1

My very dear friends, Jeanne and her late husband Bob Brenton, started the Grand Old House. They built it up to be one of the finest in Cayman. Jean loves to cook, getting up in the wee hours of the morning and proceeding to create! Her freezer and refrigerator are overflowing. If there is a disaster, I know where to head, for months of gourmet eating!!

I enjoy cooking sometimes, as well, and Jeanne and I have spent a lot of time discussing recipes.. She reminded me that in the early days, when she would get a recipe from me, I would tell her, "You know I always leave something out"..She says she will never forgive me. I have loved the red roquefort they served at the Grand Old House and she has given me the original recipe. However, I had to swear a blood oath never to give it out. Anyway, we try to eat a heart healthy diet and the original recipe does not qualify. So here is my version of Jeanne's recipe.

1/2 C. honey
4 oz. veg. oil
6 oz. ketchup
1/2 tsp. garlic salt
1 Tbs. Dijon or Grey Poupon mustard
2 Tbs. lemon juice
1 Tbs. Pickapeppa
4 oz. crumbled Roquefort cheese or Blue cheese

Just put all ingredients in a bowl and mix, adding the Blue cheese at the very end. It is a great taste!! this is about 4 servings.

Red Roquefort Dressing #2 or 'Honey Bear' Dressing

This is Jeanne's original recipe, handed down from her mother, exactly how it's written on her recipe card.

8 oz. honey
4 oz. vegetable oil
6 oz. catsup
4 Tbs sugar
garlic salt or powder: 6 shakes
salt: 4 shakes
1 tsp Colman dry mustard
2 Tbs. lemon juice
6 drops Lea & Perrins

Mix above ingredients and add 4 oz crumbled Roquefort or Stilton cheese or amount desired.

Papaya Dressing

Papaya is nature's tenderizer and this would be good for marinating meat as well. The papaya is also nature's cure for indigestion.

1/2 C. oil
1/4 C. lime juice or red wine vinegar
1 Tbs. papaya seeds
1 Tbs. honey
Salt & pepper to taste.

Whir in blender until mixed.
The seeds may be dried and put in a grinder mill to use as a tenderizer or pepper seasoning too.

side dishes & veggies

Fran's Wild Rice

This is a tribute to my High School chum's mom, Fran Seagraves.... It is delicious!!

1 C. wild rice
3 C. bread pieces or crumbs
1 C. chopped onions
1 C. chopped celery
1 tsp. sage
2 tsp. parsley
1/4 C. margarine
1 1/2 C. chicken bouillon

Wash rice and cook 20 min. in 4 qts boiling water. Meanwhile sauté, celery and onion in margarine and add parsley. Combine bread and rest of ingredients and add bouillon. Cook until liquid is absorbed, or bake at 350* for 15 to 20 min. and serve.

Barbecue Onions

8 onions peeled (med size white onions are best)
1 C. barbecue sauce
a pinch of cinnamon

Cut onions in half, place in glass dish, cover with a good barbecue sauce, cover with foil, put in oven and bake at 350* for about 30 min. or put into microwave, cover with plastic wrap and microwave about 8 min. until done. about 4 to 6 servings.

Kris and I clowning around as usual.

Maybe now that all of my family have the recipe, I won't have to always, 'bring the beans!'

Baked Beans

This is one of my favorite foods. It is also an inexpensive staple, the thing to have for a Barbecue, at Easter with Ham, or a good old fashioned family gathering. This first recipe was my Aunt May's family recipe and calls for Lima beans: 2 C. raw dried lima beans, add 2 qts. water & soak overnight. In the morning simmer until tender. Drain, place in earthen pot, if available, otherwise in large covered pot. Take 1/2 lb salt pork, scrape rind, cut into small pieces, bury in the beans, or ham hocks, or raw bacon. Mix.

1 1/2 tsp. dry mustard
2 t. cumin
2 basil leaves or crushed basil
1 tsp thyme
1 tbs. Pickapeppa
1 tsp. salt
1 Tbs. wine vinegar
1 chopped onion
3 chopped garlic cloves
1 tin stewed seasoned tomatoes
1/4 C. molasses
2 Tbs. sugar   Pour over beans, add enough bean stock to cover
1/2 ketchup   beans, cover pot & cook 6 to 8 hours. Remove the lid,
1 C. bean stock   for the last hour, but do not let beans dry out.

and here's a shortcut favorite of mine. I must confess I only usually do this one now. Despite the long list, it is easier...

1 can black beans
1 large tin of B & M baked beans
1 tin baby lima beans
1 tin Great Northern white beans
1 tin chili style kidney beans
1/2 C. good barbecue sauce
2 Tbs. Pickapeppa sauce
2 tsp. dry mustard
pepper to taste
1 large white onion
2 C. chopped celery
1 C. chopped green pepper (if available)
2 to 4 crushed garlic cloves or garlic seasoning
2 to 3 Tbs. olive oil to brown onion, celery, & garlic cloves.
1 Tbs. cumin
2 tsp. black pepper and or a touch of scotch bonnet sauce, (if desired)
Brown onion, garlic, & celery in pot, add rest of ingredients, draining some of the liquid off, but reserve it to keep beans moist. Simmer gently until flavors blend, adding reserved bean liquid as necessary. Adjust the recipe to your liking of beans & vegetables, however do not eliminate the cumin... throw in a handful of basil and serve...

Two beautiful granddaughters, Teri and Erica, up to no good in my kitchen.

Black Beans, Cuban style

Healthy and delicious black beans should be a staple in everyone's home.

2 lbs clean black beans (rinsed in a colander)
1 whole crushed garlic bulb
1/2 green pepper chopped
1 small jar pimientos
1 C dry sherry
1 bay leaf
a handful of chopped fresh basil leaves
1 can tomato sauce (optional)
1/4 C Spanish olive oil
Salt and pepper to taste
1 tsp of Scotch Bonnet sauce
2 tsp cumin
1 large onion chopped

Soak overnight. Next day boil beans & bay leaf for one hour until soft. Saute garlic, basil and pimientos, and onions; pour in tomato sauce and stir. Add mixture to beans and add sherry. Let beans thicken at low heat, about one hour. Some people like to eat it over rice..... Of course, you could just open 2 cans of black beans, add ingredients and simmer. You should always serve with chopped onion and sour cream either as a side or on top.

Cassava 'Cuban Style'

As cornstarch is made from Cassava, this makes its own thickening. I hate peeling the fresh cassava, so I use the frozen cassava. Do not defrost, but plunge frozen cassava into boiling water, return to a boil and slow down to medium and cover. When nearly cooked, check water and uncover, you need to reduce water to about half, remove some. Add crushed garlic and some margarine or butter, salt and pepper, a touch of lime juice, stir. Continue cooking on simmer until water turns pasty and into a thickened sauce. If in a hurry, sometimes I just use the Garlic salt with parsley, instead of reg. salt and fresh garlic. It is just as good with no detectable taste. Keep stirring to get sauce flavor through the cassava. Serve as your starch dish.

The Cuban version is to mix the garlic, butter and lime together separately and pour over cassava when serving. The authentic "yuca con mojo" is done separately. Cook cassava separately and make the Mojo to pour over when ready to serve

    1 C. olive oil
    2 C lime juice
    2 med onions sliced
    10 cloves garlic

Combine lime, onions, and garlic in a skillet and saute adding the oil, add 2 Tbs of the cooked juice of the yuca and whisk into oil mixture..... Pour on top of yuca when ready to serve.

The Bergstroms from Wisconsin on a visit to the Cracked Conch!!

Eggplant Haitian Style

This is a delicious, easy, fast, and healthy way of preparing eggplant, a very "good for you" vegetable. It was prepared in a similar way at a beautiful hotel in Haiti some years ago. All I can remember was that the owner had two Lamborgines..... and Baby Doc invited myself and my son Jim (then 10 yrs old) to his residence the next day to see his motorcycles... An opportunity I am kicking myself for not having taking!!

1 eggplant
1/2 to 3/4 C. sauteed onion
2 garlic cloves or garlic salt (optional)
3 Tbs. tomato sauce
Optional to add a little salsa if you like.
Sautéed mushrooms are also another variation that make it delicious.

Peel a med. size eggplant cut into chunks, boil until tender. Strain into bowl and mash with a mixer. Add about 1/2 cup chopped sautéed onions and garlic, and 3 Tbs. tomato sauce, mix well. Place in a casserole dish, sprinkle parmesan cheese over the top. Bake in a 340* oven for about 15 min..

Puerto Rican Style Eggplant

A wonderful couple in Culebra, Puerto Rico, prepare this everyday and say it is the secret to their good health!

1 eggplant,
1 tomato
3 smashed garlic cloves
olive oil
about 1/2 C. onion

Peel eggplant, lightly brown onion and garlic in oil, add chopped eggplant and chopped tomatoes, salt & pepper to taste. Cook on med. until tender about 15 min. and serve.

Fried Milk

This has to be one of the most unique and "heavenly" things I have ever eaten. I had this dish in Trinidad many years ago, but they wouldn't give me their recipe. A friend, Ray Smith from Grenada, got it for me, It took him a year. From "The Birds Nest" in Grenada:

> 5 or 6 egg whites
> 1/2 tsp salt
> 1 1/2 Tbs corn starch
> 3/4 C milk
> 1/4 C frying oil (a light oil)

Beat egg whites with salt until saucy and stiff, not dry. blend corn starch and milk and fold into egg whites. Heat oil, in deep fat fryer, add egg mixture and cook quickly, until thick and fluffy. Serve at once.

Variations, Crab meat, 3 Tbs sherry and 1/4 tsp. ginger , fold in crab meat mixture when blending corn starch and milk. Shrimp, Lobster or shredded ham can be used instead of crab meat and for my taste forget the ginger. Serve in a nest of deep fried rice noodles.

Leslie's Pasta

Daughter-in-laws are a blessing; both of the ones I have can really cook and they bring fresh new dishes to eat. This one is a favorite.

> 1 lb sharp grated cheddar cheese and 1 lb mild grated cheddar cheese
> 1 16 oz pkg bowtie pasta (can substitute)
> 2 tins cut up tomatoes (Italian or Mexican seasoned is great)
> 1 Tbs sugar
> 1/4 C. butter/margarine
> salt & pepper to taste
> 2 tsp. oregano and basil
> 1/2 C fresh cut up parsley (if available) or 1/4 dried parsley

Boil pasta, spray 13x9 baking dish with oil, mix all ingredients in bowl and pour into dish. Bake at 350* about 20 min. until pasta starts to brown on the edges. The bit of crunch is what makes it so good.

Hot Potato!!!

In 1963 as we opened the Tortuga Club, our custom made tables made out of Spanish maho were not completed. Therefore they were not shipped, and as is the normal practice when living on an island, we had to make do. We put up several construction horses with pieces of plywood on top, covered them with a tablecloth and served dinner family style. As our staff was inexperienced and I was inexperienced, we were tying very hard to get it right. One of my pet peeves is cold food served warm and hot food served cold.... Hot food must be hot and cold food must be iced down and served cold. We were having a problem as there was a bit of a walk to the dining room from the kitchen and food could cool down. I had expressed my intentions of the food being hot this particular night and that is all I could think about even though I was the hostess at the table. The food was brought in, my husband was speaking with the first guests, which consisted of our parents and a few adventurous people. The potatoes did not look hot. I cannot believe to this day, that I did what I did to the horror of all. I jumped up, with my finger, jammed it out of sight into the middle of the mashed potatoes! My husband shouted, "What are you doing!!!" and I replied in the matter of a general shouting " Attack!": "They are cold!" and with that I whisked them back to the kitchen until they were replaced with hot potatoes! Never again was hot food served warm!

Sweet Potato & Mashed Potato Supreme

My stepson Rene' can really cook--this is his contribution to Thanksgiving or Christmas.

    1 large can of sweet potatoes; save drained juice
    equal amount of mashed potato
    orange or pineapple juice
    marshmallows

So easy and delicious. Beat sweet potato, adding about 1/3 C. of orange or pineapple juice, if any more liquid is needed, use saved drained juice from sweet potatoes. Blend well. Put into a rectangular cake pan, bake at 350* for 20 min. When ready to serve, cover with marshmallows, put into oven and bake at 400* until marshmallows are melted and browned. Of course some pecans and coconut might add a bit of pizzazz!

Grandkids Sarah, Lucy, and Jay

Plantain Casserole

8 slices boiled ham
6 very ripe plantain
4 beaten eggs mixed with 1 tsp. salt & 1 tbs. milk
1/4 C. grated parmesan cheese
1 C. cheddar cheese cut in pieces
string beans
boil fresh or frozen green beans until done, then drain.
fry 3 strips of bacon until crisp, along with
!/4 C chopped onion,
2 tbs. green pepper
add 1 tbs. tomato paste
(mix all together for layering in casserole)

Cut plantain in medium diagonal slices and fry in hot oil, turning until lightly brown. Drain on paper towel. Spray an oblong glass casserole dish and arrange a layer of plantain, a layer of the prepared cut green beans, a layer of ham cut in strips, and some of the cheddar cheese. Repeat layers until you finish with a layer of plantains. Cover with the beaten egg mixture and sprinkle with the grated parmesan cheese and margarine. Bake at 400* for 20 min. A delightful lunch or dinner dish! Serves about 8, no leftovers!

Rudiger's Mushrooms

This is a dish that Rudiger Czeranka used to serve at the Cayman Arms, many years ago. Gourmet magazine wrote him for the recipe and he sent it to them. He gave out copies to his friends, and I am grateful for being included in his list. Rudiger was a tall Austrian, he could really cook! He had a sarcastic quick wit and depending on your mood, could be very humorous! At times he was quite insulting and people went there just to "jostle" wits with him. He left the Cayman Arms and went to the Lobster Pot, working there until ill health forced him to stop working. He passed away shortly there after.

Sauce:	Mushrooms:
1 1/2 tbs butter	4 tsp. minced onion
2 tbs flour,	2 tbs butter
1 to 1/2 cups scalded milk	1 lb mushrooms
1/2 C. dry white wine	1 tbs soy sauce,
nutmeg, salt, & pepper to taste.	2 tbs brandy
	4 slices French bread
	grated cheddar cheese.

In a sauce pan melt butter, stir in flour, cook roux over low heat, stirring for 3 min. Remove pan from heat and pour in the scalded milk, whisking vigorously, add wine, until the sauce is thick and smooth. Add nutmeg, salt and pepper to taste, simmer for 15 min.

In a skillet saute onion in butter until translucent, add sliced mushrooms, saute for 1 to 2 min. just tender. Remove the pan from the heat, add soy sauce, warmed brandy, ignite and shake pan until flames go out. In each of 4 ovenproof soup bowls put 1 slice of toasted french bread, divide themushrom mixture amount the bowls, top with the sauce, put on grated cheese. Bake 12 to 15 min. until cheese is bubbly. Serves 4.

A few options: 2% milk, wine and cornstarch to eliminate a lot of fat. I use Pickappa instead of soy sauce. Also, after slicing the mushrooms I like to squeeze a little lime juice over them, so they keep their color. I like to do things ahead of time, so I can visit with my guests.

Rice

My husband loves rice and it is healthy and can be delicious. Perfect Fluffy Rice. Secret; 1 C. converted enriched, white rice, 2 1/2 C. water, pinch of salt, a touch of olive oil (love to use the garlic olive oil). Put into a heavy bottom pan with a good tight lid, bring to boil, give a good stir, and put on the lid. The secret is to have faith... Do not remove the lid until the 20 min. timer rings.... It should be perfect. If not, put lid back on for an estimated time. To keep, after cooking, put clean towel on top of pan and replace lid, to prevent it from becoming gummy.

We have switched to brown rice, and it takes longer but works on the same principle. The bran is still on the rice, Converted white rice is stripped of bran, yet is enriched with vitamins.. I love to stick things into the rice to make it taste better; onions, garlic, vegetables, etc. A lot of times I use bouillon instead of just water, or sometimes, a touch of dry white wine.

The Old Tortuga Club under construction in East End in 1963.

Caymanian Rice and Peas

1 16 oz package red kidney beans, wash & soak over night.
2 tins coconut milk
1 C. each: chopped onion, green pepper, & celery

Boil beans until tender, add rest of ingredients, and 2 C white rice, turn down to simmer, add salt, pepper, and thyme to taste. Cook 30 minutes, covered. If you lift the lid during cooking it will not be so perfect......
Serves about 6 to 8 people.

I do not know why the beans are called "peas" except that in the old days they used a dried "pigeon pea" that looks like a bean. Whatever....

My Grandson Jay has eaten rice and beans since he could chew, basically he has existed and grown up on rice and beans and he looks great!

Risotto

2 Tbs. lite olive oil
1 C. arborio or ambra rice
1/4 C. tomato paste or French Tomato Sauce (in book)
1/2 C. wine
1/2 C. onion,
1 to 4 crushed garlic buds to taste
5 C. chicken bouillon or other stock, (stock from shrimp and lobster shells is excellent.)

A total of 5 1/2 C. stock /liquid to one C. rice. Brown chopped onion and garlic in hot oil, put in rice and slightly browned. Add liquid, a little at a time, stirring constantly, adding more after absorbed, until all liquid is used, about 20 min. Put in the final touch like adding slightly sauteed, shrimp, lobster, and scallops at the end.

Variations may be numberless.. again, mushrooms, any fresh veg. can be added in small amounts. Parmesan cheese can be added at the end, before serving.

This photo was taken in 1965 at the original Tortuga Club during the first performance of Byron Lee and the Dragonaires from Jamaica .

Rice Pilaf

Add seasonings for a Pilaf, at the beginning. Put in vegetables, unless they are too soft or only take a little cooking. Curry, saffron, or other seasonings. Add chicken stock, bring to rapid boil. Variations, Tex Mex rice; add cooked kidney beans and jalapeno peppers. Oriental type, add ginger, garlic, raisins, scallions, and cashews. Let your creativity run wild!

Cho cho

This is a very interesting light green vegetable, in the squash family. There are many various names in the Caribbean and I did fall into an embarrassing situation in Puerto Rico, at a convention, saying "I loved cho cho", after I was prompted into the 3rd repetition, a friend whispered the meaning of those words in Puerto Rican and I was red faced and devastated... However, I am from the western side of the Caribbean and we call it cho cho... It is also known as christophine or chayote. The tender skin and large seed, with distinctively flavored flesh, are edible and nutritious. Its flavor is delicate and it can be used in meat dishes and seafoods, cooked in any number of ways. As squash, sliced raw on an appetizer tray, it can be a point of interest. It can be marinated in an oil and vinegar dressing and used in salads. I remember one time I could not come up with a dessert in the old days, and we used the reliable cho cho as apple slices in an apple pie recipe and it was outstanding!

Some suggestions to prompt your creativity!

1. Steamed and drained, sliced or diced looks pretty along with carrots, buttered, with salt and pepper.

2. Can be used as a shell container base for stuffing with crab, lobster, etc. by steaming until tender. Remove the seeds and a little pulp and then, stuff them.

3. It can be scalloped by layering with onions, peppers or other vegetables, with a cream sauce with or without cheese, it can be a very different and delicious vegetable dish. It can be a color accompanyment if you throw in a little red bell pepper or some sliced pimento pieces.

My mom, Violet Keen, or 'Nana' as the kids called her, or 'Jonee' as her friends called her, always loved the old Tortuga Club. Here she is fourth from left.
From left, Uncle Walter, Aunt May, Barrie, Mom and Lew.

As the ever-resourceful Caymanians have found, there are many uses for the abundant plants and trees that grow here—aside from the obvious culinary purposes that we've already talked about...

Gum, Glue & Kites

A sticky tale;

Well now, gum; yes, the old fashioned Island way of making chewing gum... One sunny day, I was taking a ride with Bob Soto and Kem Jackson, when we came upon a naseberry tree laden with lovely, round fruit resembling the irish potato. They were just waiting for us to pick them so we jumped out and began savoring the delicious naseberry, a relative of the larger sapodilla. The milk and unripe fruit is called chicle which is used to make chewing gum. The fruit is delicious and if you should get a chance to eat some one day, please do so! They taste a bit like a pear but are smaller and sweeter. The naseberry is easy to eat with only a few smooth black seeds to slow you down along the way. After the three of us got back in the car, Bob and Kem told of the sap which they had used as chewing gum years back when they were boys. They would chop into the bark of the trunk or a large branch which was used for healing wounds, and gather the sap. They would dry it about two hours or overnight, and then "rake a ball" of it and mix it with brown sugar. It was the best gum they ever chewed! They also used the sap for glue when they made kites, using it fresh from the tree, spreading easily and setting up quickly. As boys they had decided that there were three trees that made the best gum: the Naseberry tree and the breadfruit tree. What fun it must have been to discover this!

So If your kids are getting lost in the TV or computer games, sitting on their backsides and complaining about having nothing to do, take them on a trip to days gone by and try making some chewing gum while weaving a tale from the past!

Another fun activity that occupied many of the children, long since grown, was kite flying. Since kites were not yet readily available, leave it to innovation to find a way...

Recipe for kites: In the past, a few stores carried large rolls of white or brown thin paper about 30" wide, which were cut to wrap groceries. Children would take a piece of this thin paper or, if they were lucky, they had received a present covered with Christmas wrapping paper which they saved just for this purpose. Today's kids will also enjoy kite making, as store bought kites are expensive and making your own always lends a sense of accomplishment! First, cut thin paper in kite shapes with 6 points. Next, take a branch of a coconut palm frond and strip the fiber from the main stem. Cut it into 3 pieces to make the shape of the kite you want to build. Lay them out on a flat surface and allow to dry for a couple of days. Arrange the fibers in your kite shape, laying one strip over the other. Tie them together with a thin cotton line, trimming the tips of the 6 points to the size you want. Next, tie a thin line to the tips of the cut stalks bringing the ends together to pull the stalks into shape. Then you are ready to glue the paper to the outlined frame of the kite. After gluing (with either tree sap or its modern day equivalent, white glue), let it dry until stuck firmly. Now attach a nice tail made from your mother's old slip and attach your father's fishing line, rolled up and fastened securely on a stick. Go fly your kite and hope your father does not want to go fishing!!

seafood

Cooking Fish

My original idea of fish was, not to eat it.... However, after moving to the Caribbean, having the "fish market" at my door step, hearing and reading all the health benefits, and making an intense study of Caribbean and international recipes.. I am now a "Fish Lover". It is delicate, easy to chew and to digest, very quick to prepare. There are many suggestions I will offer here in developing your enjoyment of fish.

First suggestion, stick with fillets. Fish bones are tiny and sharp and frankly, unpleasant in my mouth! Yet, on the other hand my husband gets a great deal of pleasure out of savoring a fish head. The best fish stock is made from fish heads and we make soup and stock from them at the restaurant.

We deal mostly with grouper, snapper, dolphin (not Flipper, but the fish dolphin, spanish name "dorado" or becoming more popularly known as Mahi Mahi), wahoo, tuna, etc. Do not turn your nose up at shark; well cleaned when freshly caught, the strong fishy odor is avoided, and shark steaks can be very delicious.

Some quick methods of cooking fish are to prepare the fillets, rinse them in water, and add a little vinegar or lime or lemon juice, if you feel it has a fishy odor. Pat the fillets dry. I like to season them with lime juice, pepper and garlic salt or fresh crushed garlic and sliced onions. If I am going to sauté them, I add a touch of Pickapeppa sauce. To blacken them I put on blackening seasoning, put on the presprayed grill to avoid sticking, make sure it is hot and cook very quickly, depending on the thickness, 1 min. each side on a hot grill is enough for 1/2 " fillets. You want to retain the moisture. I have kicked myself many a time by getting distracted... many times by, "Honey, where is the ....." by you know who.... You can use a barbecue grill with a rack, or a pancake griddle, which is the one I prefer. Sometimes the fish breaks up on the grill rack.

If you want to sauté, you might want to dip in seasoned flour, and cracker crumbs, and sauté just until meat is white and tender. Remove from pan immediately or it will continue to cook even while off the heat. You can spray the pan with a cooking spray, or opt for a some olive oil, but butter is the best.

With a little of the crushed garlic and sliced onion it is very nice. If you want to simmer gently, add a little dry white wine (about 1/2 C), touch of dill weed and chopped fresh parsley. Be creative, add a couple Tbs. of the French Tomato sauce, or throw in some mushrooms when you put in the fish, or do the fish, remove with a slotted spoon, and quickly do sliced mushrooms and zucchini. Sometimes I use chopped fresh basil, parsley etc.

Baking takes about 20 min. depending on the size of the fish. My husband does this beautifully and it never tastes as good as when he prepares it. He usually does a whole fish, cleaning it, washing it well. He seasons it with salt, pepper, Pickapeppa, a touch of my Scotch Bonnet sauce. He makes slits in the body of the fish sticking in chopped onions and green pepper. He slices fresh tomato on top and sometimes he will put butter or margarine on top and completely wrap in foil and bake at 350* for 1/2 hour or longer depending on the size of the fish. Any kinds of fresh vegetables can be used, such as mushrooms, zucchini cut in strips, etc. **Bon appetit!!**

Cayman Style Fish

This is a staple food of all Caymanians. There are varying opinions of the use of ketchup, but it is so good.

1 lb fish fillets about 3/4 to 1" thick (mahi mahi, snapper, or grouper)
1 Tbs lime juice
1 C water
1/2 C thinly sliced onion
1/2 C sliced green or red bell peppers (or both for color contrast)
1/2 C diced tomato
1 Tbs. Pickapeppa (worstechire sauce can be subtituted)
1 Tbs. ketchup
1/4 C butter or margarine

Marinate fillets in lime juice and water with salt and pepper for about 15 min. Pat the fillets dry. Heat 2 Tbs of the butter in a nonstick skillet over moderately high heat until the foam starts to subside. Add the fish and saute, turning once until just cooked through, one to two minutes. Do not over cook, this dries out the fish and ruins it. Saute fish in small amount of butter or margarine. Remove fish from pan, leaving the juices from the fish, adding a little more butter as needed and saute the onion and bell pepper until soft, adding the tomato, pickapeppa, 1 Tbs ketchup, 1 Tbs lime juice and simmer until flavors are blended, about 2 min.   Put fish on a plate and pour the sauce over it. Serves 2 people.

Coconut Fish or Shrimp

A very simple and easy meal to prepare. Always impressive!

Mix 1 egg and 1 C. water
Mix 1 C flour to 1/2 fine corn meal
Have oil hot, use when drop of water sizzles
1 C shredded coconut

Rinse fish or shrimp in lime juice and water, dip each piece in egg mixture and then into shredded coconut, then into flour mixture. Fry briefly in hot oil. Most people over cook seafood. The fish and shrimp just needs to be light brown, then removed and put on paper towels to drain.

Conch Stew

This is one of the old time staples. It is one of my favorite foods!

5 lbs. conch
3 strips crispy fried bacon crushed
2 to 3 coconuts to 5 to 6 C. water or 2 tins coconut milk, with 4 tins water
2 green peppers
3 onions
2 tsp. black pepper
2 Tbs. Pickapeppa
3 Tbs. margarine or oil to fry onion & pepper
2 tsp. thyme
1 green or red bell pepper chopped
Salt to taste under 1 Tbs.

Pound conch very well, slice, put into cooking pot, cover with coconut water adding more water if needed to cover, & scald, bringing to a boil and simmer about 20 min., till tender. Mix with other ingredients, cook about 40 min., add "pie" (tiny dumplings) on top, simmer till cooked.

"Pie" or homemade noodles; About 2 C. Flour, water, & salt for pie.

"Pie": Mix flour, a little salt, and water until you have a nice workable dough, kneading a few times. Pull off a piece about the size of your whole thumb. Flatten out by placing between two thumbs and forefingers to flatten, then lay on top of slightly bubbling stew. Some locals roll the pie into pieces the size of your finger, it makes me think of worms, I hate it rolled! This helps to thicken as well. Another variation is to add a touch of tomato ketchup... This version you can skip!

A delicate and delicious meal when it's prepared properly. It is a delight and one of our most popular dishes at the Cracked Conch This photo shows cracked conch, conch fritters, and marinated conch. It's the 'Conched Out Special'!

Cracked Conch

1 lb conch fillets
1 C flour
1 C cracker meal
3 cup water
3 eggs

Conch is a wonderful mussel, similar to clams, with its own distinctive flavor. The meat is white and fleshy. However, to prepare it properly for cooking, it needs to be tenderized. After cleaning the conch steak it can be pounded down until it is about 1/2" thick, this is the secret, if you do not pound properly it can be tough! So it is worth giving it a couple more "cracks" with the mallet!

Mix egg & water together in a bowl. Mix cracker meal and flour in another bowl. Dip conch in egg & water and then in mixed flour & cracker meal, lightly. You do not want to coat it too much, and deep fry for about 1 1/2 min. or 2 min. until lightly browned. Serve and dip in our classic tartar sauce.

Other preparations are to take the tenderized cracked conch steaks seasoned with Pickapeppa, lime juice, salt and pepper and sauté' quickly in butter or margarine. Serve with butter and lime over the top. Serves two people.

Easy Bouillabaisse

This can be a treat, the combinations are your choice.

1 medium onion, sliced
1 Tbs oil
1 tsp. fresh pressed or chopped garlic

2 large 28 oz cans tomatoes, cut up, with liquid
1 can minced clams, with liquid

Choice of any or all fish, fresh or frozen:
1/2 or more lb. grouper, yellowfin tuna, dolphin, shark, snapper
1 doz. mussels
1 doz. shrimp
trimmings from 1 head & tail of salmon, boiled & cooled for stock (optional)

1 1/2-2 C white wine
1/2 lb. scallops (optional)
1/2 lb. crabmeat or crab flakes
1 or 2 4oz. jars chopped pimientos

1-2 loaves French bread, depending on size

Saute onion til transparent- add garlic and cut up tomatoes & clams &
liquid. Cut all fish into bite-sized chunks, and put into pot - plus shellfish.
Cook on Med.-Med. Hit 15 minutes or until simmering, uncovered.
Add wine, scallops, cut up crabmeat and drained pimiento.
Cook, covered, 5-1 min.
Serve w/ French bread to pass. Serves 6 or more, and re-heats well.

If you like, add 1/2 packet Old Bay Seasoning (or 1 T), and /or 1-2 fish
bouillon cubes, and pepper to taste. The whole recipe is very flexible and, after
sauteeing the onions, can be cooked in microwave or stove top.

Fish 'N Coconut Milk

A delightful and delicate way to serve fish.

2 lb. fish fillets
3 oz. butter
1/2 pint coconut cream/milk
Cut fish into pieces

You may dip fish in coconut cream then in a small amount of flour, salt & pepper to taste, (or leave plain) sauté in margarine and until golden brown on both sides. Add coconut cream and simmer for 2 min. Serve with glazed carrots or any of your favorite vegetables and starch.

Serves about 6 people.

Fish Roe

An absolute delicacy! This calls for snapper roe, but similar fish roe can be prepared the same way. The roe looks like two kidneys attached with membrane. Slice through membrane to make two pieces. You are unable to peel off the membrane, as the miniature eggs will fall to pieces. So put each piece down and gently flatten it out. If you slice it open long ways down the side that was attached to the other side... , it will flatten and divide into two more pieces, giving you 4 nice servings. Season with plenty of lime juice, a little garlic salt, pepper, Pickapeppa Sauce. Cover and put in fridge for at least 1/2 hr. Fry up some bacon, drain bacon and save drippings to cook roe in. Cut up 1 med. onion, some green pepper (if you like it), and cook until translucent, add roe steaks, and press down with a spatula when putting it in the pan, as membrane tends to pull upward, if it breaks now it is alight. Cook until light brown and translucent roe turns white. Turn over, pressing down and cook other side. Steaks should be about 1" thick. It only takes about 3 min. for whole cooking. It is a terrific treat!

Some recipes recommend wrapping roe, putting it in the oven, and cooking until done. I do not like it dried out.....   Hope you will enjoy it as well.

Bob in Little Cayman filleting a fresh catch.

Fish Rundown

This is made with whole fish, as the fish head is what gives the best flavors. However, for speculate fish rundown eaters it is better to use fish fillets... Put into a pot your "breadkind (cassava, potato, local yam,)" onion, green pepper, 1 tin coconut milk and 1 tin water, bring to a gentle boil, and add local style heavy dumplings* simmer covered for about 20 min. add seasoned fish fillets, simmer with lid on for another 15 to 20 min. until fish is flaky.

--Dumplings; 1 C. flour, 1 C. corn meal, a little sugar, pinch of salt. Mix and knead to a firm dough. Makes about 6 flat like dumplings from this amount. I prefer softer American dumplings.

French Fish Sauce

Excellent to steam fish in and to season other dishes. I had a French friend who would keep a batch in the fridge for constant use!

    5 or 6 crushed garlic cloves
    1 onion, chopped
    2 fresh tomatoes or 1 - 16 oz. can tomatoes
    1 tsp. paprika
    1 tsp. Mexican chili pepper

Brown onion and garlic, put in blender with rest of ingredients and blend, simmer on low about two hours.

Garlic Lobster

Similar to Lobster Suzanne but not as much trouble.

    Diced peppers & onions
    10 oz. lobster
    Salt and pepper
    White wine (about 1/3 C.)
    Cream (about 1/3 C.)
    Garlic (about 3 crushed buds)

Sauté lobster until half cooked. Add diced vegetables & garlic. Sauté until meat is cooked, deglaze with white wine, add cream, reduce to proper consistency. add a little salt and pepper to taste.

Exact measurements are not given, but I have estimated approx. measurements. Adjust to your preference as to garlic, cream, and white wine. Do not overcook lobster or veg. We stuff back into lobster shell and serve that way. Can be served with rice, pasta, stuffed baked potato, or inside a mashed potato ring(my preference). I have ceremic scallop shells and I put the lobster inside and "tube" the potatoes around the edges, as I do in the Lobster Suzanne recipe. Serves about 4.

Oven Fried Shrimp

    2 doz. large defined raw shrimp
    2/3 C. flour
    1/2 C. beer
    1 tsp. poupon mustard

Prepare shrimp, season with salt, pepper, dip in batter, place on Pam sprayed cookie sheet bake in 450 oven 12 min., or until shrimp looks done, Do not overcook.. You can add shredded coconut to batter, which makes it a little special. If you wish to deep fry them, go ahead!!

Lobster Suzanne

This is an elegant dish and works well by being ready for last stages of popping in oven for a few minutes before serving. It is a recipe which Gourmet Magazine requested and I never answered.....Now I 'm sorry about that!

    4 C. lobster meat about 4 tails
    4 C. cream sauce
    1 small finely chopped onion or 6 chopped shallots
    2 C. fresh mushrooms
    1 tsp. salt, dash of pepper
    a pinch of dill
    2 tsp. Pickapeppa sauce
    2 oz. sherry
    2 oz. brandy
    Grated sharp cheddar cheese

Cook lobster gently, do not overcook 1 second! Remove from shells and chop into 1" pieces. Make cream sauce, sauté onion or challots, and mushrooms, just until onion is translucent & mushrooms are done, add sherry. Put together with cream sauce. You may stuff back into lobster shells or use scallop dishes, At serving time, cover top with shredded cheese and put into over at 350* just until cheese is melted and starting to brown, serve.   If using scallop shells, I like to put a ring of mashed potatoes around the shell. This looks great and is the right amount of a starch. While the cheese is melting the potato ring turns slightly brown and is a filling meal with a colorful vegetable. Add a light salad and this makes an elegant presentation.

    This will make about 12 individual servings in scallop shells. It is rich, but very delicious.

for the cream sauce:
    6 tbs. margarine,
    6 tbs. flour,
    2 C. reg. or 2% milk
    2 C. Carnation cream

    Melt margarine, add flour mix until absorbed, adding a little more margarine, if necessary. Remove from heat slowly add cream & milk, stirring constantly. Place back on heat and stir until thickened. Set aside until ready for use. Generally will thicken as it cools, adjust the liquid as needed.   6 to 8 people.

Cold Fish with Avocado Sauce

1 large onion cut in thin slices
3 med. crushed garlic cloves
1 C. sliced carrots
1 C. sliced celery
2 Tbs. chopped parsley
1 Bay leaf crumbled
Pinch each of thyme, oregano, salt & pepper.
1/2 C. lime juice.
2 C. water.

A whole fish, snapper, grouper, tuna, etc. makes a nice presentation, however, nice firm fairly thick fillets can do just as well with less trouble. Put into pot all the ingredients, bring to a boil and turn down to simmer for about 10 min. Remove from heat and add cleaned fish whole or fillets and turn down to the lowest simmer. Cover and gently steam fish just until cooked through maybe 10 min. for fillets, longer for a whole fish. Do not let pan go dry, add more liquid as necessary.

This can be prepared the day before and chilled in refrigerator. Drain liquid before serving.

Avocado Sauce

2 ripe avocados
3 Tbs. lime or lemon juice
1 Tbs. finely grated or chopped onion
pinch of salt and pepper
3 Tbs. lite olive oil
a touch of Scotch Bonnet sauce to taste

Put in blender, blend until smooth, cover with plastic wrap, patting down to lay directly in contact with the avocado sauce, which prevents it from turning black. This can be served on the side or on top of the fish when serving.

Salt Fish & Ackee

Both of the recipes on this page are really staples from Jamaica and have a huge following.

1 lb. salt fish should be soaked from the day before, washed, with salt removed or boiled with water thrown off each time, I recommend 3 times, continue until water is not too salty. Simmer until fish is flaky (about 20 min.). Remove bone & skin.

4 strips bacon fried until crisp, drained and broken into pieces.
1 C. chopped onions
1 tsp. pepper sauce
1 tin of drained akee (about 1lb tin or 1 full cup fresh akee)
pinch of thyme
pinch of black pepper
1 ripe chopped tomato

Cooked chopped onion, tomato, add fish, turn until heated through, then carefully add akee, turning gently until cooked through. Serve with fluffy white rice.

Salt Fish Balls

3 C salt fish, soaked from day before; boil and throw off water at least 3 times to remove salt, adding fresh water each time.
3 C pumpkin cut in cubes (can substitute hubbard or winter squash)
2 eggs
salt & pepper to taste
2 C soft bread crumbs

If salt is not out of the fish, boil and throw off water about 3 times, then simmer until fish flakes easily, about 20 min.. Drain thoroughly. Remove skin & bones. Boil pumpkin about 20 min., until tender, drain and mash with hand mixer, add margarine, and rest of ingredients. The mixture should be thick to holds its shape in the spoon, If it too thin, beat in up to 1 C. bread crumb a tablespoon at a time until you can form the ball in your hands. Roll fish ball in remaining crumbs, fry in hot oil over med. heat until browned, not burned, then turn and drain. Serve hot!

Seafood Pasta

A real hit with pasta fans. So versatile, you can be creative and use any of your favorite seafoods.

10 oz. lobster cut up
2 C. shrimp
2 C. calamari (sliced) or scallops
1 tbs. margarine
3/4 C. chopped onion
3/4 C. chopped green pepper
2 C. sliced fresh mushrooms
1/2 C. heavy cream

Put onion & green pepper in a glass dish with a little water to wet bottom, cover & microwave for about 1 1/2 min. until veg. turn translucent. Sauté lobster & shrimp just until about done, add calamari, & mushrooms, cook for about one min. longer or until seafood turns white & mushrooms are tender. Add salt & pepper to taste. Add white wine to glaze about 3/4 C. simmer gently, pour in heavy cream and cook down, serve on linquini.

For a red sauce,
Sauté onion, 3 crushed garlic cloves, green pepper, some basil, thyme, salt & pepper to taste, pour in 1 12 oz. tin whole tomato (I like the "Mexican style" tinned tomatoes) & 1 small tin tomato paste, simmer 1 hour on your lowest heat. Prepare the above recipe and instead of adding wine & cream add the tomato sauce.

For a short cut.... Buy 1 16 oz jar of chunky spaghetti sauce without meat and add that.... It is fast & easy, also I like a little of my scotch bonnet sauce & a touch of Pickapeppa.. This then becomes Linguini Diavalo.

**Fish can be added to the seafood medley as well and one of the others left out. For a real quick meal, try real or imitation crab, & lobster can be used just adding to the sauces, as they are already cooked. Both of these are great products and can make you a really fast, rather elegant dish.

Whole Baked Stuffed Fish

This can be a beautifully presented dish. You can fancy up the name... Use any of the regular, tender, white meat fish, snapper, grouper, dolphin, tuna, kingfish, wahoo, etc. Have fish cleaned well and skinned. Soak fish in water with lime, lemon, or vinegar, about 1/2 hour. Rinse well, season with salt, pepper, crushed garlic (optional), chopped onion, any fish seasoning you like, or adobo, touch of dill, oregano, thyme, basil, etc. Use Pickapeppa & seasonings all over inside and out! Make sliced green pepper, and tomato slices on top and wrap in foil. Place in a baking tin, with sides to catch any of the juices. Bake until fish is flaky, about 45 min. depending on the size of the fish. Serve with the delicious gravy!! No need to drizzle hollandaise over it, but that would be a rather fancy, fattening addition. Serve on a platter with a potato or rice ring around it.

The following three recipes are all variations on a theme of the great layered no fail shrimp and cheese combo...

Shrimp & Cheese Fondue

Not a real fondue, but the flavor is great!

6 slices bread
3 eggs or 3/4 C Egg Beaters
1 cup milk
1/2 tsp mustard
1 tsp garlic salt
1 tsp pepper
1 tsp paprika
1 C cheese sauce
2 C shrimp pieces (canned or fresh)
1/2 C chopped onions
1/2 C chopped parsley

Place slices of bread in 13" x 9" rectangular pan or glass dish, Mix next 6 ingredients, cook chopped onion in microwave until translucent, add to mixture with fresh chopped parsley. Add cooked shrimp to mixture and pour over bread. Pour over cheese sauce adding a touch of Pickapeppa, and Tiger Sauce, or salsa if you like it a bit spicy. Bake at 350 until set. Serve with salad.

Shrimp & Cheese Strata

Easier and less worry than a souffle about "falling", and the flavor is great !

8 slices day old bread, trim off crusts
6 slices American or sharp cheese or 2 1/2 C. grated sharp
cheddar cheese
3C. milk
4 eggs
1 tin cream of shrimp soup
1/2 tsp. dry mustard
1/4 tsp. salt
1/2 tsp. pepper
1 tsp. paprika

Place 4 slices of bread into 10" x 10" square pan or oblong casserole dish sprayed with Pam. Cover with sliced cheese, cover cheese with remaining 2 slices of bread, top with 2 remaining slices of cheese. Mix next 6 ingredients, beat well, and pour over bread and cheese. Let stand for about 20 min. Bake in 350 oven about 1 hour or until puffed and brown.

Shrimp Strata:
2 C. shrimp pieces fresh if available or a combination of fresh & canned
1 tin cream of shrimp soup
1/2 C. chopped onions
1/2 C. chopped parsley
1 C. mushroom slices, fresh or canned.

If you wish to make it a fancier dish with shrimp, saute' onions, mushrooms, until translucent and shrimp until just opaque, and add parsley. Pour half over first layer of bread, and the rest over the second layer. You may also add a touch of Pickapeppa, Tiger sauce, or salsa if you like it a bit spicy. Sprinkle with paprika, bake at 350 until set. Serve with salad.
Serves 4 to 6 people.

Snapper with Mango Sauce

2 Tbs. butter or margarine
1 lb fish fillets, prepared with salt and pepper
1/2 C. Mango Chutney
1 ripe banana
2 Tbs. lime juice

Sauté' fish fillet in melted butter just until it turns white; never overcook. Depending on thickness, about 1 to 2 min. each side. Remove.
Without wiping out the pan, put in the mango chutney, the sliced banana, and the lime juice. Heat quickly and pour over the fillet and serve. If you wish, you can also bake this dish.

Fish "Meuniere"

Soak boneless & skinless fish fillets in milk for 3 min. Roll in seasoned flour and fry in butter until golden brown. Remove fillets to a serving dish. Pour off fat from skillet and add fresh butter heat until light brown and pour over the fillets. Garnish with parsley and lime wedges.

Snapper Meuniere

A delicious French style of preparing fish, which to me is the best. Have fish fillets cleaned and ready to cook. Dip the fillets into flour with a pinch of salt & pepper. Quickly brown fillets til crispy, in butter; remove from heat. Melt butter and combine with lime juice then pour over fish right before serving.

Sauteed Meuniere

Follow same recipe, except omit milk soak, use lime juice, pickapepper, and a touch of my pepper sauce, marinate in this for 30 min. drain & dip in flour. Fry in butter remove and pour over the fresh melted butter & serve. You can use margarine as well.

Snapper Supreme

Take fish, prepared as in Meuniere, but don't put on butter and lime juice. Cover with sauteed sliced mushrooms and grated light cheese of your choice, put under broiler until melted, then add parsley on top and serve. These simple uncomplicated methods are really the best.

80

Suzy's Time Savers, tips and tricks...

Measuring butter
Measuring hard butter, margarine, or shortening: When you need one cup, use a two cup measure. Put in 1 C water, add butter until it comes to two cups, then dump out the water. This is a great trick which makes measuring a little simpler and faster.

Pie Crusts
Wax paper is a must for rolling out pie crusts. Use a piece on top and one on bottom, slightly dampen counter so wax paper will not slide, put down wax paper, flour lightly to prevent dough from sticking. Put dough in middle, pat down a little, and place top piece of wax paper on top, roll out to desired thickness and shape. Works well for other types of dough as well.

Too Much Salt
Something in the pot too salty? Cut a potato in half and put it in the pot, cooking 15 to 20 min. Remove potato, it absorbs some of the salt.

Sugar Lumps
To soften brown sugar lumps, put in a jar with moist paper towel under the lid, or heat microwave oven briefly. Don't put the lid in the microwave.

Crying Onions
Peel onions under water to keep from "crying". Or place matches in your mouth, with sulfa end out, do not light! Better yet, get your husband to chop them.

Betsy's Laundry Pretreating spray
1/2 C ammonia and 1/2 vinegar. Spray on before washing. Simple. Cheap!!

Turtle Steak

Turtle steak is a delicacy, and needs to be prepared properly. It is expensive and hard to get, but delicious.

    1 lb turtle steak
    1/2 onion
    1 C fresh mushrooms sliced
    1/2 C heavy cream

Tenderize the turtle steak by using a tenderizing mallet, turn steak over and pound other side. Lightly salt and pepper, then sauté in butter until lightly browned, (do not overcook). Remove turtle steak, Put in onion slices and sliced fresh mushrooms, adding more butter if necessary, in same pan. Sauté, adding about 2 Tbs. coconut rum, about 1 min. Add about 1 Tbs. each, Pickapeppa sauce, Tabasco or Lea and Perrins and about 1/4 to 1/2C heavy cream, depending on amount of turtle steak. Add turtle, simmer 2 min. until thick and a nice gravy has formed. This recipe is for about 1 lb. of turtle steak or servings for 2 people.

Turtle Linguini
This same recipe can be used for turtle pasta, except you would need to cut the turtle steak into strips, sauté adding a bit more cream and pouring over linguini. I would also add fresh pea pods when sautéing the vegetables.

The old Tortuga Club
East End

Conch Loaf

Great for a family meal because it can be prepared ahead of time.

4 conch steaks ground or finely chopped
1 chopped green pepper
1 chopped onion
1 tsp. salt
1/ tsp. pepper
1 tsp. bell pepper sauce
2 tsp lime juice
1 Tbs. parsley flakes
1 pinch thyme
1 pinch dill weed
1 C. oat meal
1 C. bread crumbs
1 can cream of mushroom soup
1/2 C. ketchup
1 egg

Mix all ingredients together, put into a meat loaf pan, patting down firmly, & bake 1 hour at 350* until done. Serve with boiled breadfruit or potatoes or anything.. macaroni and cheese would be great too!

Crab Cakes

2 Tbs butter
2 Tbs chopped onion
1/2 C. soft bread crumbs
1 beaten eggs
2 Tbs mayonnaise
3 C. flaked, chopped crab meat

1 tsp dry mustard
1 Tbs chopped parsley
1 tsp paprika
1 Tbs Pickapeppa
scant tsp dill weed

Saute lightly, onion, and bread crumbs in butter. Add rest of ingredients, mixing thoroughly. Chill for 2 hours, Shape into cakes, about 4 oz each, 1 1/4' thick. Dust lightly with flour or bread crumbs. Saute on both sides until golden brown and cook on medium for about 5 minutes.

Cleo and Frank

In the beginning years of Tortuga Club, I had a very interesting interview. A very sturdy tall lady came to the Club to apply for a job cooking.

She was 39 years young, had never worked out before, only at home, caring for her elderly parents. She had ridden a bicycle for the first time, to get up there and had fallen off on the sand road! She came to the bar area and we sat on two stools and spoke with each other. Cleo said: "I am not used to taking orders from anyone." I said, "Well you would have to take orders from me, but I would always explain what had to be done and why." Cleo said she would give it a try and I agreed on a trial period of 2 weeks. I thought that anyone who had gone through what she did to see about a job, she sure deserved a chance. She was, and is, a fabulous cook and a wonderful person, with a natural gift of cooking. She is still there going on 45 years!

Her brother Frank came to work there as well. He started out as a bartender and ended up managing for me and the owners after I left! I am sure they were Heaven sent and helped me through many tough years and loved my children as though they were their own! Frank's two wonderful children were very close to us as well.

The original staff at The Old Tortuga Club in East End. Head chef and matriarch, Cleo, is on the extreme left.

chicken

Chicken Breast fillets

Chicken dipped into egg or egg beaters and then fresh or packaged Parmesan cheese, fry or bake in oven. They are delicious. How's that for a "no brainer"??

You can use any chicken (thighs or breasts) with the skin on or skinless.

Chicken Fajitas

6 boned & skinned chicken breast halves, sliced into strips.

Marinade:
2 crushed cloves garlic,
1 1/2 tsp cumin
1/2 tsp salt (optional)
3 Tbs lime juice,
1 Tbs. Pickapeppa, toss with some blackened seasoning.
Pour marinade over chicken and refrigerate at least 30 min.

Tomato Salsa:
2 chopped tomaoes,
1 small chopped onion,
1 fresh chili pepper, sliced thin,
1 Tbs fresh lime juice.   Combine salsa and refrigerate.

Vegetable Melange:
1 large onion, sliced,
2 garlic clove, minced,
1 green pepper, sliced,
1 yellow or red sweet pepper, sliced
1 Tbs olive oil

Saute' vegetables in olive oil until soft, do not overcook, set aside. Take out chicken and put on grill, using an oil spray to prevent sticking, cook quickly, tossing to cook thoroughly. Warm tortillas as directed on package. To assemble each tortilla, layer vegetable mixture, cover with chicken, top with tomato salsa. Some like to add sour cream & guacamole on top, actually the fat free Blue Cheese Dressing does it for me, and the dish stays healthy. Even a little black bean dip gives it a boost. Calories per serving: 212, 6 grams fat, without the additions. Serves 4.   8 reg. size tortillas

Chicken N' Dumplings

Golly, I just got a letter from a lady who said I prepared this dish for her 30 years ago and she would like the recipe.... I checked the cookbook and I had forgotten to put this in it!! So here it goes, my mom's recipe..

One whole chicken or 6 chicken breasts skinned, or thighs. whatever.
water to cover
carrots chopped, or small whole baby ones
1 onion chopped
about 2/3 C celery chopped
2 to 4 chicken boullion cubes, being careful about adding too much salt
1 tsp poultry seasoning or some thyme, basil, oregano
1 tsp garlic salt or more if you like, or fresh crushed garlic
dash pepper
Bisquick

Cut up one whole chicken, or cut other breasts smaller, put into pot, bring to boil, and turn to simmer. Add onions, carrots, celery, and seasonings, cover. In the meantime mix up double the recipe for the bisquick dumplings, so easy, just use recipe on box for dumplings. You can mix in some parsley flakes if you like. Bring stew back up to a rolling boil and add dumplings, turn down to about half cooking heat and cook uncovered for 15 min, then covered for 15 minutes. I like to add some good frozen snow peas at the end and let sit for a few minutes until ready to serve. I also add pickapeppa for extra flavoring. You could use some Tiger Sauce to spice it up a bit. If you need to make dumplings just use 2 Tbs. shortening, 2 C. flour 1Tbs baking powder, dash of salt, 1 C. milk. Add more milk if mixture does not drop easily from spoon. Mix and drop by spoonfuls on top, but do not submerge into liquid. Sometimes I will add a can of cream of mushroom soup as part of the liquid, makes it creamier. Also I will thicken it with flour and water, if it does not thicken up itself from the dumplings. Hope you enjoy it!!

Arroz con Pollo Cubano
Chef De Guillermo

We met this very interesting and talented gentleman in Bimini while at our friends, Ken and Gayla Hall's, wedding. Earlier on in this book is the recipe for Mohitos. Well, this was the fabulous meal that followed the mohitos!! Guillermo left Cuba for Miami some years ago and built up a large food import/export business. His great hobby was fishing which he shared with many good friends, also Cubans, in Miami. We became very fond of the group and I wanted to honor Guillermo for his famous and outstanding chicken dish. So here it is!

2 chickens or parts: breast or thighs with bone or boneless, skinless, etc. Season the chicken for an hour or 2 with 3 or 4 crushed garlic cloves and 1 sour orange or lemon juice.

1/3 cup olive oil

1 green pepper
1 large onion cut up in small pieces
3 garlic cloves; crushed
1 8 oz can of tomato sauce
2 jars of pimentos
1 can of petit pois or baby peas
1 can of asparagus

3 or 4 cubes Knorr chicken broth
2 to 3 tsp salt (to taste)
1/2 tsp. pepper
1 bay leaf

enough saffron to turn it yellow
4 cups of rice
5 cups of water -
1/2 cup of sherry wine -
1 beer (Bud)

In a large pot or casserole, pour the olive oil and saute the chopped onions, green pepper and crushed garlic until the onion is a little carmelized. Add the seasoned chicken, the tomato sauce, the Knorr cubes, 1 jar of cut pimentos with its liquid, the liquid of the petit pois and the liquid of the asparagus, bay leaf, saffron, 5 cups of water, 1/2 cup of sherry wine and salt and pepper (to taste).

Bring to a boil then lower to medium heat, cover the pot and cook for aprox. 15 or 20 minutes until the chicken is cooked. Add the 4 cups of rice. Cover and cook for aprox. 30 minutes until the rice starts opening and the liquid is almost absorbed.

Add beer and stir in with a fork about 3/4 can of the petit pois. Replace cover and continue cooking over low heat until liquid is almost absorbed; aprox. 10 or 15 minutes.

The rice should be served before it dries out completely - It should be moist and fluffy but not mushy. Continue to simmer until ready to serve and then garnish or decorate with sliced pimentos, some of the petit pois and the asparagus. You can use roasted red peppers also.

My Fab Five. From left, Kris, Jim, Barrie, Sheree and Karie.

Chicken Casserole

4 chicken breasts, halved
1/3 cup lite Italian salad dressing
2/3 cup uncooked reg. rice
1 16 oz. bag frozen broccoli, carrots, water chestnuts, red pepper
or similar
1 small tin sliced mushrooms (4 oz.) Fresh mushrooms are better
1/2 C. sliced onions
1 3/4 C. water mixed with powdered Cream of Chicken soup mix for 4
Pickapeppa sauce
Adobo all purpose seasoning with cumin or poultry seasoning

Wash breasts, slice, put in 8 x 12 baking pan. Put on seasonings of choice, and Pickapeppa sauce. Pour just enough of the Italian dressing to cover each piece of chicken. Put in 400* oven uncovered for 10 min., remove chicken. place rice in chicken juices spreading evenly, then vegetables, mushrooms, & onion on top of rice. Place chicken breasts on top, pour the chicken soup mixture over the vegetables, bake 25 more minutes covered. Remove, sprinkle with Parmesan cheese, then return to oven uncovered, until rice has absorbed the moisture.

Creamed Chicken Livers & Mushrooms

4 med. chopped onions
2 1/2 C. flour
5 lbs. chicken livers
2 1/2 C. milk
1 C. margarine
2 1/2 C. water
Salt & pepper to taste (about 2 tsp. salt & 1 tsp. pepper)
1 can 8 oz. mushrooms or 2 C. fresh sliced mushrooms

Sauté onion and floured chicken livers in melted margarine. After livers are slightly browned on both sides, add milk, water, seasonings and mushrooms. Cover, simmer 30 min. Stir occasionally. May be served over egg noodles or rice. Serves about 20. Pour about 1/3 C. good sherry before stirring. It is delicious!!!

Curried Chicken

Use a cut up whole chicken, boneless chicken, or skinned chicken breasts and thighs. The latter is the healthy way. I prefer boneless, skinless thigh meat. Anyway cut into bite size pieces, season the day before by adding 1/3 C to 1/2 C curry powder (get a good curry powder) 1 med. chopped onion for 3 lbs, and 4 crushed garlic cloves, 1 T. seasoned course ground garlic salt, 1 tsp. black pepper. Put seasonings together with the meat and distribute evenly, adding enough curry powder so it is a nice yellow color. Leave overnight in fridge.

To cook, put a small amount of oil in pot, heat, brown chicken slightly, tossing, turn heat to low and let simmer for about 20 min. It will yield its own juice. At this point, you may wish to add about 1 can of plain coconut milk, however, you may opt for water and two cubes of chicken bouillon for a 3 lb. to 4 lb. chicken. I also like to add raw vegetables like carrots, cooking until done, and then thickening with flour or corn starch in a little water, stirring until thickened.

I like to serve over brown rice. Also, it is not complete without pappadums, thin wafer like circles about 8 " in diameter, that you either fry in hot oil (or I like the microwavable ones). They are nice and crispy, crunchy. The other must is a chutney, I prefer mango chutney. If you are doing this at the last minute, which I seem to do a lot, just lightly saute' your garlic and onion, mix curry powder with chicken, brown in the pot and add your liquid, bring to a boil, cut back and simmer for 40 min. to 1 hour. I throw in some frozen peas when finished and let them steam to cook for a few minutes. Then you are ready to serve in close to one hour.

This dish can be so varied, to serve with flair, serve condiments of chopped onion, tomato, raisins, nuts, shredded coconut, etc. It is better this way but my husband likes it just plain, not even with chutney, He does, however, devour the Poppadums!! Serves 4 or just the 2 of us with a lunch the next day!

The Prince and the Coffee Pot

In 1973 H. R. H. Prince Charles, Duke of Wales, was to visit the Cayman Islands. When Royalty is visiting a country, an advance team is sent to finalize plans and scrutinize the itinerary. There is much excitement as people and places are chosen to be honored by a visit or a chat to the Royal person. As the original Tortuga Club Ltd. was a unique, islandy, isolated place, we were chosen to be one of the stops on his visit.

It was most exciting and frightening. I was afraid that everything that could go wrong would and dreamed up things that did not even exist. However, the morning of the Royal visit I got it into my head that I did not have a proper pot to serve coffee in and decided that I had to go to town, over the 15 miles of marl road plus 15 miles of rough black top road to find a proper coffee pot! Off I went in our truck, I searched town and found one lovely coffee pot, but it was $500 and I simply could not afford it.

So I frantically drove back to Colliers, empty handed I prayed I had not delayed too long. I got there and jumped into the shower, only to have one of the staff shout in to me, "they are here". God I thought, they are 30 minutes early and I cannot believe I am not there to greet the Royal party!" In my haste I flew out, threw on a "bra dress", if you remember them, and ran out still "wet behind the ears", so to speak. I slowed to a demure walk when I approached the security men and was told, you are late and the Prince has been seated. The Governor then told me there was a chair by the Prince and I was to take it.... I

had not planned on this and had thought I would be serving him myself.

So I sat down and said, "I am very sorry I was not out to greet you, but you are 1/2 hour early. " Prince Charles, said, "Madam, I am exactly on time, we were to be here at 12, not 12:30." I said Oh, I apologize but I went to town to buy a proper coffee pot to serve you coffee in, and the only one I could find cost $500, and Prince or not, I just could'nt afford it! He replied, "Don't worry, I don't drink coffee"!

I said great, neither do I.

I then noticed he was not drinking his welcome libation and I had Frank make us both a drink that comes in an 8 oz glass. Frank wanted to make everything right and served us two for one in large 16 oz ice tea glasses. I believe they were banana daiquiries not of the weak variety! Thus the visit got off with a bang. H.R.H. Prince Charles was truly "Prince Charming". That evening I had the privilege of being his dance partner and he was a wonderful dancer!!! He had a great sense of 'dry' humor and a very quick wit. He was quite sincere amid all the stress of his honored position. His visit consisted of 26 other people being involved.

I sure am glad to be a commoner!

93

Sir Turtle
The Real Story

The turtle logo was originally created by Suzy Soto (formerly Bergstrom) in 1963 and sold to the Cayman Islands Department of Tourism for a token $1.00 in the early seventies.

It was used to illustrate and promote the Tortuga Club in East End which was managed by the Bergstroms, and it was Suzy who named him "Sir Turtle". Sir Turtle was a popular figure at Tortuga Club for many years and Suzy knew that she had a winner there. Soon she had tee shirts made up to say "Sir Turtle Goes Diving". They even had a Miss Sir Turtle and the reptilian couple was used to promote lovers at the Tortuga Club!

In 1970, the Tourist Board was formed and headed by Eric Bergstrom. An American by the name of Vic Chinna was hired in the marketing department and his job was to get the Cayman Islands on the map. Vic was so taken with Suzy's Sir Turtle figure that he offered to purchase the design for the use by the Government's Department of Tourism. As the Cayman Islands had limited funds available to them at that time, Suzy said she would donate her beloved Sir Turtle. The Department would not accept the logo freely so Suzy accepted $1.00 as payment. Sir Turtle was subsequently turned over to an advertising agency in Miami. They cut off one leg and gave him a pegleg. Several years later, another modified version of the logo surfaced--Sir Turtle sporting a scarf flying in the wind, which was adopted and still used to this day by Cayman Airways.

Nowadays everyone uses the popular Sir Turtle logo. He can be seen on just about every souvenir made for these islands and many businesses have modified him further to incorporate him into their company branding. Aye Aye, Sir Turtle!!

meats
(beef, lamb, pork and a few special favorites...)

Beef Stroganoff (serves 550 people)

This makes one of the nicest dishes to serve for a large group of people. It is elegant, well priced, and delicious. Good luck or bon appetit!

150 lb. beef cut in strips
288 oz. mushrooms/ 18 lb. mushrooms
12 cups chopped onion
36 qts. bouillon
3 qts. red wine
9 qts. sour cream
4 1/2 lbs. butter using more if needed.
1 qt. dill pickle
3 cups corn starch, if not enough, add more.
pinches of nutmeg and basil

Sauté onion, remove, sauté the mushrooms, remove. Sauté the beef and dill pickle, adding a touch of nutmeg, basil, salt, and pepper, sauté until tender and light brown. Mix cornstarch into bouillon and wine, stirring until dissolved. Add to meat, mixing until it thickens. Add rest of ingredients, including juices from sautéing . Mix together, simmer to blend flavors for about 10 min. Just before serving, add sour cream. Make sure not to boil after adding sour cream or it will curdle. Keeps nicely in a chafing dish; serve over about a million noodles!

Picadillo (a Cuban Meat Dish)

2 Tbs. olive oil
2 lbs. lean boneless beef (beef chuck arm roast, 3 lbs.)
1 C. onions chopped
2 cloves crushed garlic
3 green peppers seeded and chopped
1 tsp. salt
1/2 tsp pepper
2 14 oz. tins Mexican or Cajun or plain canned tomatoes
1/4 tsp. ground cloves
1/2 C. small pimiento stuffed green olives
1/2 C. seedless raisins
2 Tbs. red wine vinegar

Cut beef in 2 inch pieces place in pot, and add water to cover beef. Bring to boil and skim off any foam. Simmer for about 1 hr. for tender cuts of beef, or up to 4 hrs on a low simmer for a piece like the above chuck arm roast. In fry pan heat olive oil to fry onions, garlic, & pepper, cooking until soft. Add tomatoes & liquid, cloves, salt and pepper. Cook, stirring continuously until liquid is almost gone and the mixture is thick. Add olives, raisins, vinegar, and meat until heated through. You can add 1 tsp. Scotch Bonnet sauce, if you want a little heat. Taste for any adjustments, Serve with rice. Delicioso! Serves 4 to 6 people.

Eggplant Casserole

1 lb lean ground beef
1 med chopped onion
2 garlic cloves crushed
1/4 tsp. pepper
1 eggplant

1 can tomato pieces
1 cup cottage cheese
1 cup Ricotta cheese
1 1/4 C. grated Parmesan cheese

Saute' the ground beef, onion, & garlic. Peel & cut up the eggplant in slices suitable for layering. Place ground beef in bottom of casserole dish, and layer with tomato pieces, cottage cheese, eggplant, Ricotta, Parmesian, etc. layering twice. Bake for 35 minutes at 350*. About 6 servings, 180 calories each.

Captain Charlie

(or 'Captain Chili' as he came to be known at the Cayman Chili Cookoff!)

Well now... This book would not be complete without Captain Charlie's story.

Some years back we started a Chili Competition in Cayman. My husband and I thought we would make this a family affair and take our sons, Kris and Jim, to help cook... They were about 17 and 15 and did not want to participate in any way. We also decided to make our restaurant's mascot, Captain Charlie, the center of attention at the cookoff and renamed him "Capt. Chili". We had tee shirts made up and off we went, much to the embarrassment of our reluctant teens. I thought it would be fun if Capt. Charlie spoke about the "Wreck of the Ten Sails" up at East End and that he would tell the story of what had taken place on that sad day. So I put on a deep voice and recorded it as if I were an old sea captain. We hid the recorder and it looked authentic; as if Capt. Charlie were talking himself. Many children gathered around and began poking and pulling on Capt. Charlie to see if he was real.

This was all very annoying to our boys. Bob and I took a break and walked around to the other displays to see how we rated amongst the competition. When we returned to our booth, there was quite an audience and what Capt. Charlie was saying was, "HEY, YOU LITTLE BLANKETY BLANK..... etc". "GET YOUR HANDS OFF ME, etc. etc. etc." "LEAVE ME ALONE, @#$$%@@!!!! " and he was drawing quite a crowd. It would seem Captain Charlie had come alive and was expressing his true feelings!!!

Kris and Jim were quite pleased with the situation and were suddenly very proud to be a part of such a wonderful fun event! Teenagers!

Also, as you can see in the photo at left, I used to take Capt. Charlie in the car with me and just drive around. I'd make minor adjustments to his clothes to go with my mood or to suit

the season. I'd dress him as Santa for Christmas and as a pirate for Pirates Week. He would sit beside me in the car as a passenger and he was lovely company! I got quite a lot of strange looks, but one day, after I had Capt. Charlie situated in the car in the back seat, I ran into the restaurant for something and ended up taking awhile. A woman came running in and said for us to call the hospital immediately, as a man sitting in a car out front had passed out and was slumped over from the heat.......We all ran out and of course, it was poor Capt. Charlie, who had fallen over. Sometimes we think he gets around more than most people. Currently, he is a pirate stationed at the front of the Cracked Conch. My daughter-in-laws are pleading for his retirement, as he has seen better days and according to them, scares both children and prospective customers.

Captain's Chili

1 to 2 garlic buds (optional)
1 1/4 t. black pepper
1 t. salt
2 beef bouillon cubes
2 cups water
2 Tbs. flour
1 onion
2 tsp. cumin
1 Tbs. Pickapeppa
3 Tbs. hot chili powder
1 Tbs. oregano
2 Tbs. cooking oil
3lb chuck roast or 3 lbs ground beef.

Here we are at the annual Cayman Chili Cook Off. Note the swarthy teenager in the foreground.

The night before cooking cut a 3 lb. chuck roast into 1" cubes. Season with cumin, Pickapeppa, chili powder, oregano, black pepper, salt. Rub into meat and leave overnight.

In 2 Tbs. oil, sauté chopped onion and 2 chopped garlic cloves. Add meat and cook gently, stirring frequently with a wooden spoon till meat changes color, but does not brown. Heat 1 3/4 cups of the water with bouillon cubes and mix until dissolved. Stir into meat, let cook without lid, and cook on low with lid on for several hours or until meat is tender. Add the rest of the water with flour if it needs thickening. Optional: serve with sour cream mixed with fresh chopped parsley, sprinkle finely chopped onions.

Put a slice of lime on the side to add zip! For Chili con Frijoles... add 15 ounces of kidney or pinto beans.

This is a very delicious and impressive recipe!

Bob, Kris and 'Captain Charlie', the Cracked Conch official mascot, at the annual Cayman Chili Cook Off.

Chili Con Carne

Everybody has a favorite of this... We have a chili contest on the island every year. We never win it... Our chefs are not wearing thong bikinis, we are not "one of the boys", the chili is not so hot that you are unable to eat it, but we sure sold a lot of our chili!!!.....

   5 lbs. ground beef (get the low fat or ground chuck)
   4 C. chopped onion
   5 cans tomatoes 12 oz
   8 C. red kidney beans drained (save liquid)
   8 C. tomato sauce
   2 Tbs. sugar
   5 Tbs. chili powder
   2 tsp. salt

Brown onion in small amount of oil, brown ground beef, drain off any fat, stir in tomato, tomato sauce, reserved kidney bean liquid, add seasonings, heat to boiling, reduce and simmer uncovered 1 hour. Stir in beans, simmer another 15 minutes or until of desired consistency. You will also see our recipe for fancy chili under Captain's Chili. Serves...you guessed it, about 8 to 10 depending if you serve on rice, without, with grated melted cheese on top etc.....

Jack's Spaghetti Sauce

I have this Italian friend, Jack, from New York who married a Caymanian lady Cassie. He takes her out to dinner every Friday and then makes his spaghetti sauce during the week. He is very clever and anytime I am ready to do a project I pass it by his mind and learn all sorts of interesting things. He says his sauce is the best so here it is:

Brown beef in sauce pan, with olive oil, garlic, onions, parsley, basil, 1 can tomatoes (one big tin or two reg. tins), Cook for 1/2 hr. to 45 min, add a small amount of tomato paste, cover, simmer 3 to 4 hours, until thickened. Serve over ziti or spaghetti, with Parmesan cheese....

Lasagna

A good family favorite always served with Caesar salad and garlic bread at our house.

1 lb. lean ground beef
1/4 C. olive oil
1 C. chopped onion
3 crushed garlic buds
1 can (14oz) tomatoes (I like Mexican or Italian flavored)
2 cans tomato paste 6 oz each
2 tsp. salt
1 tsp. dried basil (although fresh is better)
1/2 tsp. oregano
1/4 tsp. black pepper
1/2 crushed bay leaf
1 C. ripe olives cut up
about 1 Tbs. Pickapeppa sauce or Worcestershire sauce
8 oz pkg. lasagna noodles
2 C. ricotta cheese
1/2 lb mozzarella cheese
2/3 C. parmesan cheese

Brown onion, garlic, and ground beef in olive oil. Add rest of ingredients and simmer. Cook 8 oz. pkg. lasagna noodles. Use 6 to 8 strips cooked lasagna noodles, drained. Use 9 x 13 baking pan, put in one strip at a time, starting with sauce spread over bottom, then a layer of noodles, sauce, spread out the following cheeses: ricotta or cottage cheese, mozzarella cheese, & parmesan cheese, then the noodles and another layer of sauce and cheeses. Do not skip the black olives as they are the secret ingredient in this dish! Bake 30 min. at 350* until done...

short cut: substitute some good prepared spaghetti sauce adding freshly cooked onion, garlic, & ground beef, & some of your favorite spices... It will taste like homemade sauce anyway. Be sure to use plenty of sliced black olives. Layer as usual & bake.

Serves about 8 and maybe as many as 10.

Salt Beef n' Beans

This is an old time favorite from a time when there was no refrigeration and salt beef was a common product. The majority of the salt was washed out; if you're still using the salt beef, you must boil and throw out the water 3 times, no less, in order to use it. Some clever ladies are using corned beef instead. It would seem the quality of the salt beef has become increasingly poor, tougher, and with more fatty tissue. The saving in time and waste is worth the extra cost of the corned beef.

1 lb. red beans (soak overnight)
3 lbs. corned beef or 4 lbs salt beef
milk from two coconuts, or 2 tins (14 oz) coconut milk
3 to 4 garlic buds chopped
2 onions, chopped
1 bell pepper
1 tsp. pepper
a bay leaf, some chopped fresh or dried basil

Soak 1 lb of red beans overnight, rinsing in the morning: cover with water and coconut milk to cover, add cut up beef, onions, garlic, bay leaf, fresh basil, Pickapeppa, and bring to boil. Turn down heat and simmer until all is tender, about 2 to 3 hours. I like mine very tender and the beans soft. Some local ladies use a little Wesson oil instead of the coconut milk, saying it gives it that flavor... I can't see it, but they are usually right!

By the way, I love this made with black beans as well as the red kidney beans. Just use the same amount.

Also, if you want the fastest route... cover your cut up corned beef with water and cook down until almost tender, add coconut milk, add canned beans, other seasonings as above, and simmer down with lid off. Pretend you've been slaving all day on dinner..If you're really desperate use a pressure cooker, but I can't help you there.

102

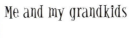
Me and my grandkids

Sauerbraten

4 lb. boneless beef roast, peppered & seasoned to taste.

1 1/2 C red wine plus 1/2 C water (this can be adjusted to 1 wine to 1 water, stronger or weaker or without any wine)

2 cups red wine vinegar
4 to 6 cloves garlic
2 med. onions
1 Tbs. pickling spice
1 tsp. instant coffee
gingersnaps

Mix red wine, vinegar, and water, put about 1 C. of the liquid in blender and quickly chop garlic and onions, then add 4 gingersnaps and blend until they are ground up. Put the liquid into a pot, bring to a boil & pour over the seasoned roast. Place in a tightly covered container and turn beef 2 times per day or once per day for 3 to 4 days. The meat is absorbing all kinds of good flavors!! When ready to cook, remove beef, drain and brown quickly in pot with small amount of oil, add marinade and proceed to bake covered, 20 min. per lb. at 340*. When finished, remove beef, take the gravy marinade, put into blender and add 2 to 4 more ginger snaps, as per taste, mix until blended. Serve as gravy. Potato pancakes are an appropriate dish to enhance this German delicacy. Carrots, turnips, etc. may also be added to the gravy when cooking, along with more onion so vegetables are cooked with roast. Serves about 6 people.

Sautéed Boemboe
(Spicy Barbecued Meat)

This recipe is similar to 'Pinchos' made with pork in Puerto Rico and barbequed outside on a chargrill. They taste fabulous.

    4 finely chopped onions
    2 cloves minced garlic
    1/2 tsp. red pepper
    1 Tbs. dark brown sugar
    1 Tsp. lime juice
    1 1/2 tsp curry powder
    1/2 ground clove
    1/2 tsp. ground ginger
    3 Tbs. water
    3 Tbs. soy sauce
    1 1/2 pound round steak, lean pork, or lamb cut into 3/4 inch cubes

Blend all ingredients together except the meat. When thoroughly blended add to cubed meat, mixing with hands to blend the seasonings. Leave in refrigerator overnight. When ready to cook, thread 5 to 6 pieces on skewers, place on broiler rack 3 " from heat, or charbroil. Broil about 15 to 20 min. Brush meat with the remaining sauce, turning frequently. Serve with peanut sauce. This serves about 4 people, but for my family of 4, I have to double the recipe!

Peanut Sauce

    2 Tbs. grated onion
    2 Tbs. olive oil
    1 Tbs. dark brown sugar
    1 tsp. lime juice
    1/4 C. peanut butter
    1 C. coconut milk (used new canned coconut milk)

Sauté onions in oil until clear. Add sugar, juice, peanut butter, blending well. Gradually add coconut milk stirring constantly. Add salt to taste. Cook slowly until sauce is thick and smooth. Makes about 1 1/4 C. sauce.

Pizza

I include pizza in my cookbook because it is one of the best all time family 'pull together' projects. Let everyone rub elbows while picking their own toppings. It's great fun and if you do it right, a great mess!

> 6 C. flour
> 2 tbs. baking powder
> 3 tsp salt
> 3/4 C. oil
> 3 to 4 C. milk

Mix ingredients and knead dough 10 times to make smooth. Roll out on floured board, into two rectangles, place on two cookie sheets. Bake at 350*, just until it starts to tan.

> Have pizza filling ready to go!
> 4 C. tomato sauce, mix in oregano, crushed garlic, pepper, etc.
> 2 thinly sliced onions
> 2 C. sliced, drained mushrooms
> 1/2 lb. sliced pepperoni
> 3 lbs. grated Mozzarella cheese
> 1/2 lb. grated Parmesan cheese

Start by spreading tomato sauce on dough. Add other ingredients, ending with Mozzarella cheese and Parmesan cheese on top. Bake at 450* until cheese is melted and serve.

There are so many great toppings you can use for pizza especially if the whole family is involved. Try different shredded cheeses, brie, goats cheese, anchovies, olives, peppers, pineapple, ham, smoked salmon, corn, proscuitto, even caviar--the sky is the limit, so let your imagination take over!

Curried Lamb

This is a very nice change for curry, but you need to love lamb.

10 lbs lamb stew meat, cut into 1" cubes
1/2 C olive oil or any cooking oil
2 1/3 C finely chopped onions
1 clove garlic
1 Tbs ground ginger
1 Tbs brown sugar
1 tsp black pepper
2 1/2 Tbs salt
1/2 to 3/4 C curry powder
1/2 C mint jelly
2 C coconut milk (about 1 whole can)
2 C Carnation evaporated milk
2 C regular milk
4 Tbs flour.

Mix ginger, sugar, pepper, salt, and curry powder with lamb cubes. Refrigerate overnight. When ready to cook, sauté onion and garlic in oil in large pot, remove and sauté' the lamb cubes. add flour and mix well. Add mint jelly, milk, and cream. Stir well, Cover and simmer 1 hour adding coconut milk last 15 min. of cooking. Serve with rice. Depending on area, condiments are served with curry dishes, I like chopped peanuts, raisins, grated coconut, grated cheese, cut up tomatoes, and cut up bananas. The amount of curry is flexible as well, depending on the heat of the ingredients. A good Indian or Jamaican curry is really good. If you do not have time to overnight the ingredients together, at least let sit for one hour to blend spices. Serve with rice. This is a really different curry and compliments the lamb very well. Serves about 8 to 12 people.

Leg of Lamb

This is one of my husband's favorite dinners.

> Leg of lamb
> 6 garlic buds
> 1 chopped onion
> Instant coffee
> 1 to 2 tsp. Scotch Bonnet sauce

Purchase a large good looking leg of lamb, defrost it and wash it off well. Trim off the fat. Prepare some (about 6) cloves of garlic, and (1 good sized onion), by slicing them in slivers. "Juke" all over with a knife making slits into which you push in the garlic and onion slivers. Take the Pickapeppa sauce and rub well into the leg of lamb, take about 1/4 C. water mixed with instant coffee, rub well into leg of lamb. For a spicy Caribbean flavor, rub in some of the Scotch Bonnet sauce, about 1 to 2 tsp. This takes away some of the gamey lamb flavor which some people object to. The coffee is really the secret ingredient which gives the gravy a wonderful flavor. Bake at 350* for the first 1/2 hour, then reduce to 325*. Bake about 20 min. per lb. and bake uncovered. When done, remove lamb, let rest about 20 min. before slicing. Make gravy with drippings left in the roaster, spooning off as much fat as possible. Mix flour and water, pepper, some thyme and basil and some more Pickapeppa, stirring and scraping the browned parts left in the roaster. Taste and add salt and other seasonings as necessary.

Serve with plain or garlic mashed potatoes or browned potatoes, (cooked with the roast) carrots and celery, or other vegetables. Popovers go well with this as well as regular dinner rolls. Serves about 6 people.

Cuban Style Roast Pig

My husband loves Roasted Pig and we finally had some Cuban friends roast him one for his birthday feast. He loved it. I still am not fond about the Pigs head being on the platter........

This brings to mind a good friend of mine, who ran a spectacular resort in Montego Bay, called "Sign Great House". He had all local staff and for his opening he told the staff to serve the pig and put an apple in the mouth and parsley behind the ears. As Jack was a bit eccentric and definite about what he wanted, the staff tried to comply with his every wish without question. The night of the opening banquet with the Prime Minister and all the officials there, the fanfare began announcing the main course with the waiters marching through with the platters held high. To Jack's horror, the waiters all had apples in their mouths and parsley behind their ears!!

Pig Roast

1 12 to 25 lb pig
6 heads of crushed garlic
6 Cups lime juice
2 Tbs. ground oregano
2 Tbs. ground cumin
Salt and pepper to taste.

Bathe the clean pig in a marinade making sure to make slits to put seasonings into the flesh. Marinate for 24 hours, belly up. Place in oven 350 * for 6 hours turning up the heat to 550* during the last 30 to 40 min. so the skin can become crispy. Baste the pig as you cook it with the marinade and juices. If you wish to cook in an open pit, turn so it can cook evenly. If you are doing a 10 lb. roast, use same procedure, cover with aluminum and roast for 3 1/2 hours. Uncover the roast for another hour until the skin is crispy. This would be for a real Christmas feast.

Pork Chops & Rice

    2/3 C. uncooked rice
    1/2 C. red wine
    1 1/2 C. water & 2 beef bouillon cubes
    1/3 C. Italian dressing
    5 pork loin chops
    Adobo seasoning
    Pickapeppa sauce
    Garlic salt

    Season chops with some garlic salt (if desired), Adobo seasoning, Pickapeppa, brown in fry pan, put on top of 2/3 C uncooked rice. Add 1 can cream of mushroom soup into juices in fry pan, stir while adding water, bouillon & red wine. Pour on top of chops and rice. Add 1 16 oz. pkg. frozen broc, red pepper, onion, gr. beans. Seal with aluminum foil, Bake at 400* for about 30 min. until rice is done.

    Seasonings like Adobo have salt, if using garlic salt do so sparingly, or substitute garlic powder. It is better to crush garlic cloves and put in pan when browning chops. To make a lighter version, substitute golden mushroom soup. This only serves my husband and me.

There really is a 'Jacques Scott'--and here he is eating pie in my kitchen with granddaughter Briana! He was our islands' most famous liquor distributor and wine connoisseur-- a VERY important man!

Our Cuban friend Roy Alvarez does all the cooking and is a great Chef!! His wife Elizabeth really enjoys it!!! Roy likes to use 1/3 C. tomato sauce, but I feel the canned tomato pieces add flavor and taste to the recipe.

Roy's Tamale en Cazuela (or my version of Roy's recipe...)

This is a Cuban favorite, my husband fondly calls it peasant food. It is meat stretched out and you must love cooked corn meal... It has been a favorite of mine and I like to head for the Cuban Restaurants in Miami to get it. This recipe is even better!!

1 lb. lean pork meat
2 cloves minced garlic
Juice of one lime
1/4 C olive oil
1 onion
1 green pepper
1 tin (14 oz) Mexican Style tomatoes
7 oz of water
1/4 C sherry
1 1/2 C corn meal
2 1/2 C water
Salt & pepper to taste
If desired, a shake of Adobo hot seasoning & my hot pepper sauce

Cut the meat in chunks and season it with garlic and lime, let marinate in refrigerator for a few hours, if possible. Brown the meat in the oil, (actually, I eliminate the oil and use a small bit of Pam, works just as well). Add minced onion, pepper, tomato and sherry. Mix corn & water, add to previously fried ingredients. Simmer on low for approx. 1 hour, stirring occasionally to prevent sticking. Serve in bowls, as a side choice. I like grated sharp cheese on top, it melts and is delicious and filling. Serve with a salad, and French bread or rolls.

For a quick version, use a double boiler, in the top, or on direct heat, boil 2 C water, slowly pour in 1 C. corn meal, stirring constantly. Bring to a boil and cook 2 min., then add fried bacon, cut up ham or cooked pork, onion, green pepper, and some fresh, fried, or canned tomato, dash of Pickapeppa, ground pepper, hot pepper, about 1/2. C. grated cheese and a little garlic salt to your taste. Place on top of double boiler, cover and simmer on low for 15 min. stirring a couple of times. Add more water if you like it softer.. Adjust either of these to your own taste and preferences.. This is good for a sort of Brunch Breakfast..... with Uncle Walter's Milk Punch!!! Find this recipe in 'Drinks'!

110

Eggs Benedict

Well now, this is one of our family's favorite dishes. Everyone makes it, loves it, and eats it!

English muffins, toasted
Slices of Canadian bacon, ham, or smoked salmon
Poached eggs not too hard, just firm and cooked on top.

Hollandaise Sauce (on page 114):
butter, lemon and egg yolks with salt and white pepper to taste.

The secret to this dish is to have everything come together at the same time so everything is hot. Usually serve two to each person. So the hollandaise sauce needs to be 1 stick or 1/2 C butter which should make almost 2 cups sauce. This should make 4 perfect Eggs Benedict, enough for 2 or 4 if one person is to get one each...that would never would work in our family.

Assemble all your ingredients. Put everything in the top part of the double boiler for the hollandaise sauce, but keep off the bottom while heating the water to a boil. In the meantime, get your English muffins split, put your Canadian bacon or your ham in the oven to heat up. (If using smoked salmon, do not heat.) Start toasting your English muffins. Spray bottom of pan to poach eggs, put in enough water that it will cover eggs and heat not quite to boiling. Break open the eggs, dropping into the water, turn down to simmer to cook slowly. Have your plates ready, put your sauce onto the bottom of the double boiler and turn heat down to about 4 (med./lo), keep stirring, cook until thickened. As soon as the sauce is finished remove from the bottom pan. Arrange muffins on plate, put on ham, then the poached egg, adding the sauce on the top spilling down the sides and ready to cut into and savor! I also like to serve fried tomatoes, or cut tomatoes in half with some Parmesan cheese on top and bake until browned at 350* about 20 min. You need nothing else with this treat.

I am sure you will also figure out your short cuts and do it your way. This sounds so very complicated but it is not, so relax, poach the eggs your way, etc. But don't miss eating this divine dish!

*for four single servings, one daughter-in-law uses four egg yolks for the sauce and poaches just the leftover 4 egg whites. Saves on the cholesterol! She has to do this because her husband eats 6 single servings in one sitting!!!

Welsh Rarebit   My Mom's great recipe!!

1 Tbs. margarine
2 1/2 Tbs. flour
1 1/2 C. milk
2 C. sharp cheddar cheese grated
1/2 tsp. mustard
Dash of Worstershire sauce
2 beaten eggs.

Melt margarine, add the flour, mix well and remove from heat, slowly stir in the milk. Return pan to low heat and when thickened add the cheese, mustard, and sauce, stir until smooth. Pour a little of the hot cheese sauce over the eggs, beating well. When thoroughly mixed, pour back into the cheese sauce. Cook another 2 min. stirring constantly. This can be served over saltine crackers, toast, with tomatoes or a deluxe version with crisp bacon over toast, with tomato and sauce on top...You may also use 1 C. milk with 1/2 C. beer. You may also add sherry if not using the beer. It is an excellent luncheon dish! This is good for 2 people in my family, might have some left for 4 total!!

1,2,3,4 White Lasagna

1. layer of cooked lasagna
2. layer using some of a jar of pesto sauce
3. layer of sauteed green /red/ yellow peppers, onions & mushrooms
4. layer of 5 oz of ricotta & 8 oz of mozzarella mixed with fresh basil

Mix up Bechamel sauce:
1/2 stick unsalted butter
3 Tbs. flour
1 1/2 C milk
pinch of nutmeg & paprika, salt & pepper to taste.

Melt butter, add flour on low heat and heat up to medium, adding milk and stir until smooth and thick, adding spices. Pour all of it over the layers above.

Repeat all of the above 2 more times, Cook 30 minutes covered at 350* & 15 min uncovered.....

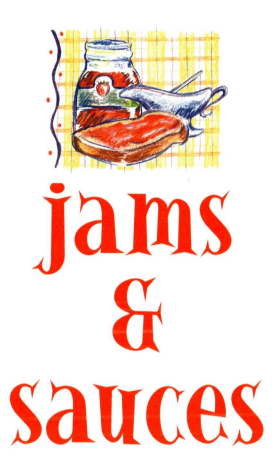

jams & sauces

Real Hollandaise Sauce

This is the cook's pride, when made properly. The variations of preparation are many. I know, as a young bride I tried making it right for one year and this is the only dish that brought tears to my eyes that eventually grew into actual crying!! I had a friend named Lucy Bell from Wayzata, Minnesota, who took pity on me and said her grandmother had the best never-fail recipe. Her family was involved in General Mills and in my heart I think Lucy's grandmother had to be the original 'Betty Crocker'... Over the years my memory has grown fuzzy, but this is close to the original recipe. We like a more limey flavor, so we use limes instead of lemon and more than the original recipe required. No one in our family can ever get Eggs Benedict that comes close to the recipe we make, as it never has the real bite to it!

Never Fail.....
　　2 sticks cold butter
　　6 egg yolks
　　1/2 C to 2/3 C lime juice or lemon juice, so start with smaller amount an adjust to taste.
　　pinch of salt

Use a double boiler, turn heat to med., bring water in bottom pan to a boil and turn down to about 3 or a low medium, put in all ingredients with cold butter cut in chunks, and stir constantly until thickened. Use a wooden or plastic spoon. Do not cook on high. If you have to stop stirring, remove from heat. Watch carefully, or it will curdle. If curdling begins to occur, you may save it by quickly putting in the blender and adding a tsp. of ice cold water and whirring on high a short time. Refrigerate left overs and reheat by adding a little hot water and stirring like mad. I have never had any left over.

Some folks like to add cayenne pepper, Tabasco, etc. I like it plain....and plenty.

Quick Hollandaise

1/3 to 1/2 C. light or regular mayonnaise
2 Tsp. lime juice
2 Tsp. Dijon or any tangy mustard
3 Tbs. butter or margarine

Put all ingredients in saucepan on med heat, only to get hot and no longer! Stir constantly and serve quickly. Increase ingredients according to taste and amount of mayonnaise you use. Do not overheat or cook. Have whatever you are going to put this on all ready, as this takes about 2 min. to prepare.

Tartar Sauce

2 C mayonnaise
2 Tbs. each chopped parsley and chives
2 tsp. chopped tarragon
2 Tbs. capers (this is your secret ingredient)
1/3 to 1/2 Cup, finely chopped dill pickle
1 Tbs. lime juice

This is a really great tartar sauce. If you wish to spice it up, add 2 tsp. scotch bonnet sauce, stir up well, taste, add more if you desire. Another variation is to add barbecue sauce to it and that makes another great tasty sauce for anything! Mix all ingredients and serve with conch fritters, fish, crab cakes, fish fritters, etc.

Garlic Butter

This is good to have on hand; save a margarine container and make with 2 cups butter or margarine.

6 cloves garlic	1 tsp. Pickapeppa
4 Tbs. chopped onion	1 tsp. salt or garlic salt.
1 Tbs. dried parsley flakes	dash of pepper

Put into blender or food processor and blend. Use on French bread or use as a spread, or a seasoning when cooking, fish etc.

Beer Batter

This beer batter is delicious. Make ahead of time and let sit.

    1 C flour,
    1 pt. beer
    1 tsp. baking powder
    1 Tbs. melted butter or cooking oil

Mix together & let sit about 1 hour. To hasten action, bring beer to a gentle boil, carefully, add everything and let stand about 15 min. Add more flour if necessary.

Another rendition:

    1 C flour
    pinch of salt
    2 egg yolks
    2/3 C beer or water
    1 Tbs. salad oil
    2 egg whites

Sift flour & salt into bowl. Beat egg yolks & beer together. Stir into flour mixture and blend in oil. Let stand 1 hr. at room temp. Beat egg whites until stiff, but not dry; fold into flour mixture.

This is really great for Fish Fingers, dipped and fried until lightly browned.

Duc Sauce

If you are serving Chinese, make a good easy duc sauce by using plum jam mixed half and half with chopped-up mango chutney. This is another really easy but effective recipe. It is delicious with egg rolls!

Wine Mushroom Sauce

    1/3 C margarine
    1/4 C flour
    2 bouillon cubes
    1 C water
    Salt & pepper to taste
    1/2 C margarine
    1 C chopped onions
    2 C sliced fresh mushrooms

    Melt margarine, blend in flour, salt, and pepper stirring continuously, dissolve boullon cubes in water and add to the margarine. Melt 1/2 C butter, cook onions until translucent, add & briefly saute' mushrooms. Mix together adding 1/2 C sherry or red wine to sauce, blending all ingredients. Serve over toast, steak, or chicken, etc. Makes enough for 6 good servings.

Mango Jam

    The first time I made this I gave my various families a small jar to taste. The next time I was making it my daughter-in-law Debbie said she would like some. I told her I needed a jar. She brought me several quart jars... now that is a real compliment!

    2 1/2 C mangoes chopped up. Try to get mangoes without strings.
    2 C brown sugar
    1 tbs. lime juice
    2 pkgs. Certo

    Mix mangoes and sugar together, bring to a boil, stirring constantly, turn to medium, and stew, stirring to prevent sticking for 20 min. or until it begins to thicken. If you have used stringy mangoes, strain it. Add lime juice and Certo, cook 3 min., cool and pour into jar to keep in refrigerator. This recipe is much lower in sugar than normal, it is great on toast, cereal, etc. Sugar is needed to thicken, but no more than 2 cups is necessary. Six cups is normally called for, and that is not healthy!

Papaya Chutney

This is the one where my gardener asked if I wanted some papaya, and I said, "sure". The next day I found 75 lbs of green papaya on my doorstep and no guests at the little hotel!! So along came this recipe and it is delicious. I also learned about the Scotch Bonnet pepper and never to touch the seeds with your fingers!!! Refer to the "story" under "Ingredients".

12 lbs Green or ripe Papaya
5 C. raisins
1 Gal. vinegar
16 C sugar
7 hot Scotch Bonnet peppers
1 C. ginger
4 onions
1Tbs. crushed garlic
 --or--
10 lbs mango
2 lbs raisins
4 qts. vinegar
8 hot peppers
1 C. ginger
8 cloves garlic
4 large onions
 --or--
16 C. vinegar
16 C. mangoes
4 C. raisins
2 lbs. onions
4 C. papaya
2 tsp. dry mustard
16 C. brown sugar
3 Tbs. salt
8 hot peppers or peppers to taste(Scotch Bonnet or your choice).
1/4 C. ground ginger
4 cinnamon sticks
12 cloves in muslin bag.

Regardless of the ingredients you choose, cut up dried fruits, peppers, add to vinegar and soak overnight. Add sliced mangoes, sugar crushed ginger, garlic, onions. Boil till thick & brown. Follow sterile canning procedures or store in refrigerated area.

PIE!!!

Pie Crusts

Pie crusts should be tender and flaky. I think the best one is made with buttery flavored Crisco, but unfortunately, I haven't seen it in years.

    1 C. flour
    touch of salt
    1/3 C. shortening
    2 tbs. water

Mix with a fork, flour, salt, and crisco until crumbly. Add water gradually, mixing until you can shape into a ball. Sprinkle a few drops of water on surface where you plan to roll out crust, press a piece of wax paper over it, spread flour in a circle on the wax paper and place ball of flour, flatten out with hand and place a second piece of wax paper with the side brushed with flour to prevent sticking. Roll out between the wax paper to size. Keep checking size with your pie pan. When size is good, peel off top sheet, then lay on 1/2 of crust. Lift bottom sheet of wax paper, folding over half the crust over the second piece of paper. Lift off the rest and place carefully onto pie pan. Unfold the top piece to fit into pan. Press down and close up any holes. Actually, this is very easy, but it is definitely the best way to get the flakiest pie crust! This is for a one crust pie. Double recipe for two crust.

**For a one crust pie, put in pie pan, prick with a fork and bake at 475* 8 to 10 min. Remove when lightly browned, cool and put in filling.

**For fruit pies, I like to use one pie crust and put a crumb crust on top. Just mix 1/2 C. brown sugar, about 3 Tbs. margarine and 1/2 C. flour until crumbly and sprinkle on top.

Just for an added interest, I have tried mixing 1/3 cup flaked coconut to the crust and substituted my favorite coconut rum and it sure was good.

Kay's Double Pie Crust

    2 Cups flour
    1 tsp salt
    1/4 C. oil
    1/4 C. milk

A good pie crust if you do not have any shortening! Mix and roll out as above.

Creative Pies

Exotic fruits. Eating in the Caribbean wouldn't be the same without them, and a creative fruit pie is the perfect finish for an island supper. There are some frozen juices that make great pies simply by mixing a 6 oz can of frozen concentrate juice with 16 oz. whipped topping, putting into a prepared graham cracker crust, and freezing.....You may also use 8 oz whipped topping and 2 /4 oz pkgs vanilla instant pudding and pie filling using using only 1 3/4 C cold milk, mixing, then adding the juice.

Others to try: guava, passion fruit, pink lemonade, etc. I just used grape juice and really enjoyed the flavor. Some may need a little more or less whipped topping, judge by tasting. This can be extremely impressive!!!

Oh yes, do not put in the fresh fruit, as it freezes also and stays frozen. Put on some sliced fresh fruit just before serving each piece, if you like! There is an Oreo cookie crust on the market, which is really good and not too high in calories at 110 per serving.

The same type of thing, but using a simple cream cheese base:

Frozen Coconut Pie

1 3 oz softened cream cheese
1 Tbs sugar
1/2 C milk
1 1/3 C. coconut
8 oz whipped topping
1 tsp vanilla

Beat cream cheese and sugar, gradually add milk, beat until smooth, stir in coconut topping and vanilla. Spoon into baked graham cracker crust. Freeze until firm, store in freezer...

Lime Meringue Pie

This is my favorite pie and my mom made this perfectly every time!!

2 C. white sugar
1/2 C corn starch
3 C. cold water
6 egg yolks
1/2 C lime juice or lemon juice

Mix sugar with cornstarch and gradually stir in water. Boil 1 min. stirring with a wooden or plastic spoon. Remove from heat and gradually stir in beaten egg yolks, stirring until smooth. Boil 1 min. longer constantly stirring, turn down heat so you do not scorch the mixture, remove from heat, stirring until smooth. Blend in lime juice, stirring to keep smooth. Cool slightly while making meringue and crust. Pour into a **baked** pie shell, cover with meringue.

Meringue

6 egg whites
1/2 tsp. cream of tartar
6 Tbs. sugar (white granulated)

Beat egg whites and cream of tartar until frothy, adding a little sugar. Continue beating until stiff and all sugar dissolved. Spread on the hot pie filling, sealing edges of crust to prevent weeping and shrinking..... Bake at 400* 10 min or until lightly brown; a short baking time at a high temperature makes a tender meringue that cuts easily. Another aid is before cutting each piece, dip the knife into cold water, shake off excess water and cut.

Egg whites sometimes throw me and I have served several desserts without the proper meringue, adding cool whip... However, there are many theories about this problem. Make sure there is no, and I mean no egg yolk in the whites! Break each egg separately into a small dish, so that if you goof, you do not ruin the whole thing. Make sure utensils are clean with no grease on them. At the beginning of the pie making, I separate the eggs and put the bowl, beaters, and egg whites in the refrigerator, while preparing the rest. When I take them out they are cool and it seems to work better. Of course you beat them on high!!!! Good luck!

Key Lime Pie

1 can 14 oz. sweetened condensed milk
1/3 to 1/2 C. lime juice (adjust to taste)
if available, some lime or lemon zest (skin peel grated fine)
3 egg yolks
1 graham cracker crust
2 egg whites
1 tsp. cream of tartar

Beat egg yolks, add rest of ingredients, mix thoroughly. Beat egg whites with cream of tartar until stiff & fold into mixture. Pour into graham cracker pie crust or a sinful crushed Oreo pie crust that has been prebaked for 5 min. at 350. Not absolutely necessary, but I like the firmer bottom. When cool, put in filling and freeze. 15 min. before serving, remove from freezer, to allow to soften if frozen very hard otherwise, you may slice and serve from the freezer.

You may add 1/2 C. sour cream or whipped topping for slightly richer versions. This is one of the original Key Lime Pies . These are often kept in the freezer and served very cold. One of our customers left a written comment that we were not serving fresh pie as it was served too cold.....“Give me a break!”

Coconut Cream Pie

A real favorite with our customers at the Cracked Conch Restaurant!

3 C. fresh whole milk or 2 % milk
2 eggs
1 C. granulated sugar
5 Tbs. cornstarch
2 tsp. flour
1/4 tsp. salt
3 Tbs. butter
3 Tbs. vanilla
1 C. coconut flakes

Mix milk, eggs, sugar, cornstarch, flour, and salt, and bring to a boil on low, stirring constantly, until it thickens. Add rest of ingredients. Put into a 9" pie crust (either graham, or regular crust prebaked.) Chill and serve with whipped topping and toasted shaved coconut sprinkled on top.

This is our new talking, moving animatronic 'Captain Charlie' that now graces the front lobby of the Cracked Conch. My daughters-in-law were screaming for the retirement and proper burial of the old 'Captain Charlie' on the grounds that he was beginning to scare small children and destroy customer's appetites.

Dirt Pie

This is one of our best sellers at my Restaurant!. One of my competitors, a dessert expert says, "it is the best I have ever eaten"! Now he will know how easy it is!!

      1 C. cold milk, 2% milk cuts down calories & fat
      1 4 serving size jello Choc. Instant Pudding /Pie Filling, sugar free if you want to cut sugar intake
      8 oz. Cool Whip, chocolate is great, white one is fine too.
      8 choc. Oreos crushed
      1 1/2C. (rocks) made up of your combination choice of granola, small choc. chips, chopped nuts, pecans, walnuts, etc.
      1 graham cracker crust

Use granola chunks, choc. chips, chopped nuts, or combo. Pour milk into bowl add pudding, beat until well blended. 1 to 2 min. Let stand 5 min. Fold in whipped topping, stir 1 C. of crushed cookies and 'rocks" into mixture. Spoon into pie crust, sprinkle with remaining cookies, freeze until firm, at least 4 hrs. Remove to refrigerator about 2 hour before serving. Put cool whip on top or whipped cream... It is fantastic!!

Shoo Fly Pie

This dish came from the Pennsylvania Amish. It is a breakfast pie that goes with coffee and is out of this world. We have it every Christmas morning.... While the pie is cooling, is when you will need to say "Shoo Fly", as it smells so good, attracting all kinds of "flies"!.....thus the name!!

1 egg beaten
3/4 C. black strap molasses or regular molasses
3/4 C. hot water (not boiling)
1 tsp. baking soda

Beat egg in bowl and add molasses. Get hot tap water and stir in baking soda to dissolve then add to molasses mixture and stir until frothy.

Crumb topping
3/4 C flour
1/2 tsp cinnamon
1/2 tsp salt
2/3 C light or med. brown sugar
2 bs. margarine
You may add a pinch of nutmeg and ground cloves, but I prefer this plain.

1 9" unbaked pie crust

If you like a sticky moist bottom, put 2 Tbs of molasses on bottom of crust and spread out. Reserve 1 cup of the crumb topping. Add remaining crumbs to the liquid mixture and pour into the pie crust. If you want a tasty variation, you can add 3/4 C pecan halves spread out over the molasses before pouring in remainder of ingredients. Sprinkle rest of crumbs on top. Bake 375* for 10 min. and 350* for 30 min. until knife comes out clean. Let cool a bit before slicing.

My Mother wrote this for me some years ago and it struck a bullet in my heart, and I am thankful to have it to pass on to my daughters.

Looking Beyond

For myself I do not mind the growing old;
The change comes slowly and I do not notice
The little at a time.
My waistline spreads and is a trifle loose, but I accept it
As another birthday adds a year.
The joints are stiff, and veins show like oval hills;
My skin is potted from the dots of middle age.
My walking slows, but if I forget and pace too fast...
I find myself breathless again, but for another reason;
That another season passed, but rich with memories
Warm and long, and laughter and dividing joys.
Now it is for my daughter that I mind;
She will look at me and notice the etchings of
My life upon my face,
Her thoughts will spin on until they reach herself;
She, too, one day will be the same
As the mother she beholds,
And seeing me, my daughter may look - and be afraid.

By my mother, Jonee Keen.

special cookies

Ahhh...Cookies!

Is there really any other cookie, other than Chocolate Chip? (Maybe the Peanut Butter Cookie...)

Chocolate Chip Cookies

There are so many recipes for this classic cookie, however, the original was first on the radio on "Famous Foods from Famous Eating Places" in 1939, sponsored by General Mills. Of course, Betty Crocker! Credit is given for the invention of the Toll House cookie which was developed by Kenneth and Ruth Wakefield and named after their lovely New England Toll House on the outskirts of Whitman, Massachusetts.

The original recipe has been doubled, so you can freeze part of it, bake all of it, or eat some of it raw. I must admit I have a hard time getting it baked, when I chill it, I confess to eating a great share before I get it all baked. (You can imagine my excitement when culinary geniuses came up with Chocolate Chip Cookie Dough Ice Cream!)

Cream together:
> 1 1/3 C. soft margarine, butter flavored shortening
> works, but no more than half.
> 1 C. brown sugar (packed)
> 2 eggs
> 2 tsp. real vanilla extract

Then add:
> 1 scant tsp. baking soda
> 1 scant tsp. salt
> 2 1/2 C. all purpose flour or 3 C. sifted flour
> 12 oz. chocolate chips or c.c. mini morsels (I like these better)

Bake at 375* 8 to 10 min. Lift off immediately onto wax paper, to prevent any further browning on bottom of cookie.

Cupcakes With the following changes, you can make a super cupcake:

Just change margarine to 1 C.
Use baking powder instead of soda (2 tsp.)
Use 4 eggs
Add 1 C. milk
increase brown sugar to 1 1/2 C.

Mix in the same manner, again using 12 oz pkg. Spoon into greased and floured muffin cups, 3/4 full. Makes about 24. Bake at 375 for 18 to 20 min. Use your favorite frosting. I like the coconut/pecan caramel one, already in a plastic container in the frosting sections. I would recommend putting some of it in a microwavable dish and adding some water to cut the sweetness and to lessen the fat content before spreading on the cakes.

Congo Squares

This recipe is from a woman I greatly admired. She had 12 children, a good home and a wayward, handsome husband. She was extremely kind and nice to me as a very young married girl. She gave me this recipe around 1957. I treasured it and made up the recipe many times, which was enjoyed by my five children and a host of their friends! I like to freeze them and sneak one, especially on a diet!!!! It gives me a great upturn in spirit and I believe this is one of the comfort foods the psychologists talk about! Here it is;

2 C. sifted flour
2 1/2 tsp. baking powder
1/2 tsp. salt
2/3 cup butter or margarine
1 lb pkg. of light brown sugar or 2 1/4 cups.
3 eggs
1 large pkg. chocolate chips
2 tsp. vanilla or 1 Tbs. coconut rum (really a good touch)

Mix the whole thing together, pour into a 10 1/2 x15 1/2 x 1 1/4 greased pan. Bake at 350* for 20 to 25 min. Do not overbake as it gets too dried out. Some folks like to add chopped nuts, I add about 2/3 C shredded coconut.

129

Easy Cake Mix Cookies

An easy and great cookie that makes a truly bowl-licking batter!! Great for guests just stopping by as these things are usually inthe cupboard!

    1 box chocolate cake mix
    1/2 C. vegetable oil
    2 eggs
    2 C. chocolate chips or butterscotch morsels.

Combine cake mix, oil and eggs in large bowl. Stir in morsels and nuts, if desired. Drop by rounded tablespoons onto ungreased baking sheet. Bake in preheated oven at 350 * for 8 to 10 minutes or until centers are just set. Let stand for 2 minutes, remove to wire racks to cool.

Gladys's Scuba Bars

This is from a dynamic friend of mine, Gladys Howard, a real gourmet cook, who runs Pirate's Point Dive Resort in Little Cayman. She's from Texas and after a divorce, changed her life by exchanging some Texas land for a piece of paradise in Little Cayman that desperately needed some TLC! She has made it into one of the most popular dive resorts and people flock from all over the place to sample her Texas hospitality and scrumptious cooking. If I wore a hat, it would certainly come off for Gladys! These are so good and so easy!

    2 C. peanut butter
    2 C. graham cracker crumbs
    1 C. butter or margarine
    2 C. confectioners sugar
    16 oz. chocolate chips

Blend sugar and crumbs until well mixed, add peanut better and melted butter, saving 3 Tbs. butter to mix with chocolate chips. Combine and spread mixture into a buttered 9" x 13" pan. Chill. Melt chocolate chips with 3 Tbs. butter reserved, in microwave at half power for 1 minute. Stir, cook for 30 sec. stir again, do not overcook or chocolate will loose its gloss. Spread on chilled mixture. Chill again. To serve, cut into 2" squares. About 20 pieces.

Rice Krispy Treats

The basic recipe is:
> 6 C. rice krispies cereal
> 10 oz. bag of marshmallows or 40 large marshmallows
> 1/4 C. margarine

These treats are nice to have around to crunch on. Put marshmallows & margarine in a large glass bowl which has been sprayed with oil or rubbed with margarine, place in microwave on high for 2 min. Remove, stir, and put back for 2 min.stir again, pour in 6 C. cereal and mix well. I can never leave well enough alone and I wanted nuts without fat. Thus some of the following additions to give a nutty taste. The cereal and the marshmallows are without fat, the 1/4 C. margarine is really negligible and can be cut to 2 Tbs.. Substitute one C. of Grape Nuts, with or without raisins, really makes a treat. Here is my favorite recipe:

> 4 C. rice krispies
> 1 C. nut n' honey cereal.
> 1 C. grape-nut cereal
> 10 oz. marshmallows
> 1/4 C. margarine

Prepare as above and play around with this basic recipe. Sometimes I get a craving for sinful coconut and add 1/2 C. shredded coconut as well!

Oat Bars

> 1 3/4 C. all purpose flour
> 1 C sugar
> 1 C margarine or butter
> 1 tsp vanilla extract
> 1 egg
> 1/2 C. uncooked oats (quick cooking or old fashioned)

Beat all ingredients until well blended, put in 15 x 10 buttered pan. Pat dough into pan . Bake until golden about 1 hr, 10 min. at 275* degrees. Other things can be added, like shredded coconut, raisins, chocolate chips etc.

The four handsome Soto men; from left, Randy, Danny, Bob and Rene

Oatmeal Cookies

    1 C. margarine
    1 C. brown sugar
    2 eggs
    1 tsp. lime or lemon juice
    2 Tbs. blackstrap molasses (can substitute maple syrup)
    1 tsp. vanilla

Cream above ingredients, then add:
    2 C. flour
    2 tsp. soda
    1 tsp. salt
Mix thoroughly and stir in 3 C. oats.

    Roll into a long roll, like the supermarket raw dough refrigerated cookies. Put into wax paper and chill in fridge. Remove when ready to bake, turn on oven to 400*, remove paper, cut in slices and bake on ungreased baking sheet until lightly browned for 8 to 10 min. Makes about 6 doz.
    You can add coconut, nuts or chocolate chip mini morsels to satisfy chocolate lovers' taste buds.

Peanut Butter Cookies

Again a classic recipe, my son Kris's favorite.

    1 C. margarine or butter
    1 C. peanut butter (crunchy is great)
    2 C. brown sugar
    2 eggs
cream above ingredients then add:
    2 1/2 C. all purpose flour
    1 tsp. baking powder
    1 tsp. baking soda
    1 tsp. salt

Chill dough. Roll into 1 1/2" balls. Leave enough space between cookies to flatten with a fork dipped in flour and crisscrossed, if you don't do that, they do not taste right!!! Bake about 10 to 12 min. in a 375* oven. Makes about 5 doz. cookies. My son Kris hates the nuts, so I have to make it out of smooth peanut butter. Can you believe that?

Snow Ball Cookies

These lovely light cookies are one of my daughter Sheree's favorites and I used to make them every Christmas, along with Shoo Fly Pie. Making any less is a waste of time as everyone loves them!!!! Now, Sheree makes them!

    4 C soft margarine
    2 C sifted confectioner's sugar
    4 tsp. vanilla
      9 C all purpose flour
    1 tsp. salt

Cream first 3 ingredients, add the rest, then decide on using dough as it is, or adding chopped nuts or coconut. I like the addition but my daughter Sheree likes them plain! Chill dough. Turn on oven to 400* Roll into 1 1/2" balls. These do not spread, so you can bake closer than normal cookies, on an ungreased baking sheet, just until set, not brown. While still warm, roll in confectioners sugar, cool and roll again. Makes about 9 doz.. These do not last, and again are delicious 'raw'...

White Chocolate Chip Oatmeal Cookies
by my high school chum Susan Stomp

These are by far the best cookies I have ever eaten! Susan and I get together once every 12 or so years... The last time was in Marsh Harbor, Bahamas! She is great and has not changed except for the age thing we all fight. We snorkeled, laughed, reminisced and when Susan went to bed I snuck into her kitchen, into the refrigerator, and into her tin of the best chocolate chip cookies made with lots of oatmeal-- so they had to be good for me, right? Right!!! I could not stop eating them. Anyway, they are my comfort food and I usually make a batch when the other one gets low!

The single batch recipe is:

1 C. butter
1 C brown sugar
1 egg
2 tsp vanilla
1 tsp baking soda
1 C flour
3 C regular oatmeal (my preference) (quick 1 min. can be used)
2/3 C shredded coconut
8 oz white chocolate chips (you can use regular choc. chips also)

Cream butter, brown sugar, egg, and vanilla. Add flour, soda, mix well, add oatmeal and coconut, mix well and add chocolate chips. Mix together. I prefer to put a light cooking oil spray on the cookie sheet. I like to press my dough flat, and Susan likes to leave hers as they fall on the cookie sheet from the spoon. Either way is good, but by flattening them they are a bit crispier. Bake for 10 min. in a 170 oven. Yield is about 40 small cookies.
Now you might as well double the recipe, and if you do 12 to 16 oz of the chips is fine. This can vary according to your taste. Also you can use different margarines, they give a slightly different texture but frankly, they are all good!

The original staff of the old Tortuga Club in East End

80 is Better

A prominent Chicagoan reached his 80th birthday and this is what he said about how it feels to be 80:

I have good news for you. The first 80 years are the hardest. The next 80 years is a succession of birthday parties. Everybody wants to help you up the steps and everybody wants to carry your luggage.

"If you forget your name or anybody's name, forget to keep an appointment or promise to be in two or three places at the same time, spell words wrong, spill soup on your necktie, fail to shave on one side of your face, or if your shoes don't match or if you carry a letter around for a week before mailing it, it is all right, because you're 80.

You can relax with no misgivings at 80. You have a perfect alibi for everything. Nobody expects much of you. If you act silly it is your second childhood, everybody is looking for softening of the brain.

Being 80 is much better than being 60 or 70. At that time they expect you to retire to a little house in Florida and become a discontented grumbling has-been. But if you survive till you are 80, everybody is surprised that you are still alive, surprised that you can walk, surprised that you can reveal intervals clearly.

At 70 people are mad at you for everything, at 80 they forgive you for anything. If you ask me life begins at 80 and not at 40. At 80 you have learned that 'inch by inch life is a cinch, yard by yard life is hard'"!

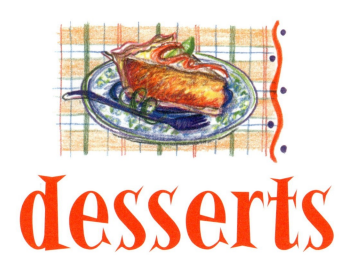

desserts

Debi's Banana-Chocolate Chip Cheesecake

My daughter-in-law"s delightful recipe for the best, most sinful cheesecake you will ever eat!!

3 8oz pkgs of cream cheese (softened)
1 C. white sugar
2 tsp vanilla
3 eggs
1 C sour cream
2 bananas
6 oz milk chocolate chips

Mix cream cheese, sugar, vanilla until smooth. Beat in eggs, one at a time. Blend in sour cream, bananas, chocolate chips. Pour into crumb crust and bake at 350* for 60 to 70 minutes.

Crumb crust

You can buy the prepackaged graham cracker crust or Oreo cookie crust. Here is the recipe for the Oreo cookie crust:

1 Pkg reg size Oreo cookies
1/2 stick or 1/4 C. butter / margarine

Crush cookies in blender and pour into pie pan, sprinkle with butter and mix with fingers, press against sides and bottom for crust and bake 10 minutes at 350* . Let cool completely and then chill for at least 4 hours. Below is a sour cream topping for the final touch!

Sour Cream Topping

Beat 1 C dairy sour cream, with 2 Tbs sugar and 2 tsp vanilla until blended. Spread over the Pie, and sprinkle grated chocolate on top, before cutting and devouring!

Cheesecake!!

A variety of cheesecake recipes have flooded the market...One of the easier ones:

Creamy Baked Cheesecake

1/4 C. margarine melted
1 C. graham cracker crumbs
1/4 C. brown sugar
2 8 oz cream cheese, softened
1 (14 ounce can sweetened condensed milk)
2 eggs
1/4 C. lime or lemon juice
1 8 oz. sour cream

Preheat oven to 300* Mix margarine, crumbs, sugar in pie pan, pat firmly into pie pan. Bake 5 min. to crisp crust a bit. Beat cheese till fluffy, beat in milk, and eggs until smooth. Stir in Lime juice. Pour into pie crust. Bake 50 to 55 min. at 300*

White Chocolate No Bake Cheesecake

1 pkg 8 oz cream cheese softened
2 pkg white chocolate pudding mix
2 C. cold milk, divided
8 oz whipped topping thawed

Beat cream cheese and 1/2 C milk, add remaining milk and pudding mixes, beat for 1 min. Stir in whipped topping until smooth and blended. Spoon into crust. Refrigerate 4 hours. Leftovers probably could be kept in the refrigerator....but I wouldn't know because we never have any!

Cassava Cake or 'Heavy Cake'

This is an old time staple in the Caribbean. There have been some discussions as to the real origins of this type of recipe. Some believe it came from England with their various puddings. However, my belief is that it came from the West Indies, with origins within this hemisphere. The ingredients were available in abundance, with the sugar cane, cassava & coconuts, so I believe it may have come from the Carob Indians, way back. A similar one is Custard Top Corn Bread, which is really a dessert, adding corn meal and flour instead of the cassava.

3 dry coconuts* or 2 - 14 oz cans coconut milk, (low fat now available, which also works), plus 2 cans each of water (helps get out the rest of the good coconut milk). Works out to about 10 1/2 Cups liquid.
2 Tbs. vanilla
1 Tbs. cinnamon
2 tsp nutmeg
1/4 C. butter, or less & not absolutely necessary.
2 C. light brown sugar
6 C. grated cassava

Mix everything but cassava, put into a large pot and bring to a boil, and then turn down to simmer, until it separates. Skim some oil foam off top (about 1 C.) and save. Add to 6 C. grated cassava. Stir briskly and pour into well greased baking pan, 15" by 8" by 2 1/2". Bake at 350*, until set, about 20 min.. Spread 1/2 oil foam topping over it, bake another 20 min. and spread rest of topping. Bake slowly until sides let go and top is brown.

Let it cool for a day, before covering, otherwise it sweats and spoils. This way it can keep for about 5 days. Refrigeration spoils it by turning it hard. We love it with a little whipped topping.

*Coconut Milk

Put pieces of coconut in blender with very hot water, blend on high, getting the milk out of the coconut trash, pour into a bowl and squeeze coconut to get liquid out, repeat until the coconuts have been thoroughly squeezed. Put through strainer into another bowl, pressing and squeezing the rest of the milk out. Throw away the trash, and use your coconut milk.

Carrot Cake

4 eggs
1 1/2 C. cooking oil
1 C. brown sugar
3/4 C. white sugar
1 Tbs. coconut rum or rum or vanilla
2 C. all purpose flour
1 full tsp. baking soda
pinch of salt
2 tsp. cinnamon
1/4 tsp nutmeg
1/2 tsp. ground cloves
3 C. shredded carrots
1 C. chopped walnuts
1 C. raisins

Heat oven to 350*. Mix wet ingredients with mixer. Add dry ingredients, mix well, then add carrots, walnuts, and raisins. Pour in 13x9 x2" greased and floured cake pan, smoothing batter out to sides of pan so cake cooks level. Place in middle of oven for 30 min., add 5 minutes until done. Remove, let cool, and frost with Cream Cheese Frosting.

Cream Cheese Frosting

1 8 oz. pkg cream cheese, not fat free or low fat... Soften before mixing with sugar.
4 C. confectioners sugar

Begin mixing, adding up to 1 Tbs. liquid as necessary for spreading. I like to add coconut rum, but you can use cream, milk, vanilla, orange juice, etc. It will be about 360 calories and is worth every bite!!

Chocolate Mayonnaise Cake

To simplify life, use a chocolate cake mix and substitute real mayonnaise for the oil, same measurements. Prepare and bake as directed on package.

However, if you want the scratch recipe.. here it is:

    2 C flour
    2/3 unsweetened cocoa powder
    1 1/4 tsp baking soda
    1/4 tsp baking powder
    3 large eggs
    1 1/2 C sugar
    2 tsp vanilla extract
    1 C Light mayonaise
    1 1/3 C water or 1 C water 1/3 C coconut rum

  Chocolate frosting
    12 oz semisweet chocolate chips
    1 C. Light sour cream
    1/2 tsp vanilla extract
    2 Tbs unsweetened cocoa powder.

Preheat oven 350*, grease & flour one 13" x 9" baking tin. Sift and mix dry ingredients together, set aside. Beat eggs, sugar and vanilla on high for 3 min. until light and fluffy (3 min.), Blend in mayonnaise, then alternate dry ingredients with water. Pour into baking pan and bake until middle of cake springs back, but do not dry out. About 30 to 35 min.

Make frosting in a small saucepan, stirring chocolate chips over low heat until melted. Remove from heat and stir in sour cream and vanilla. Frost the cake.

This is approx. 290 calories, 14 gms fat, 5 gm protein, 41 grams carbohydrates, 218 sodium, 43 mg. cholesterol.

Flan

One night I had some Miami Cuban friends for dinner. As food and recipes are always a conversational topic, we were discussing the lovely smooth flan they had brought for dessert. The sister-in-law had made it and her brother-in-law does all the cooking for his wife. They proceeded to get into a fight over how to make real Flan....

Here was the result, two totally different recipes...

Roy Alvarez's Flan

2 C. 2% milk
1 C. white sugar
some vanilla (as he says)
4 eggs

Mix all together; in the meantime be browning (not burning) 1/2 C sugar in pan till nicely browned. Pour it in the bottom of a container you are going to use to cook the flan, pour the milk egg mixture over the browned sugar, place in another pan or pot with water in it, and bake in a 375* oven for 1 hr. This is less fattening and lighter than Virginia's.

Virginia's Flan
(the sister-in-law's version)

1 can sweetened condensed milk
After pouring out condensed milk fill same tin with regular milk or 2% milk, rinsing any of the condensed milk out at the same time.
add 1 can evaporated milk
3 eggs
"some vanilla"

Mix all together, and again do the white sugar as above and pour mixture on top of browned sugar and bake the same..... This was delicious!!

Custard Top Corn Bread

This is an "old-time favorite". It was also something my husband craved, and wanted like "my Mother used to make". Well, trying to be a good wife, I made many versions of this and spoke with many people to bring this recipe to this book!! There are many versions of this and I even found one calling for eggs. But the old timers tell me that it "never had eggs!!".

     2 C. flour
     2 C. corn meal
     2 C. brown sugar
     8 C. coconut milk (2 grated coconuts)*
     or 1 1/2 tins coconut milk + 5 1/2 C. water
     1Tbs. cinnamon
     1 tsp. nutmeg
     dash salt
     3 Tbs. butter
     1 Tbs. vanilla and or 1 Tbs. coconut rum

Prepare 6 good cups of coconut milk, add melted butter to the rest of the ingredients, stirring until blended. Pour into a 15"x8" glass or reg. baking pan sprayed with Pam. Bake at 350* for 1 1/2 hrs.. If it needs more browning on top, raise heat to 400* for about 10 min.. Remove and check. The custard should be soft and if you test with a spoon on the side to the bottom, the corn meal should be firm in the bottom, the custard soft on top; the custard will firm up somewhat upon cooling. Serve as dessert. A little whipped cream really tops off this easy but special dessert!

This was my most difficult project.. There are as many different ways to prepare this dessert as there are races of people! Thanks to all my friends who were tasters and advisors. To mention a few: Vernell Ebanks from West Bay and Cleo Conolly from East End, Annie Multon and her mom, Dina Webster from Breakers, and Olga Whittaker from Sand Bluff! Also, Olga liked her corn meal in some coconut milk before mixing because her husband likes the corn meal bottom softer!

Some experts swear you should use more corn meal than flour, some the other way around. Some add more sugar. Why not try raisins too... some variations are: 1 C. cornmeal, to 1 C. flour, 1 C. brown sugar, 6 cups coconut milk, 2 med. coconuts in a slightly smaller pan. Whatever you do, enjoy this old one and adjust to your tastes or more appropriately, to your husbands. They seem to have a lot to say, when it comes to Custard Top Corn Bread!!
*Check Ingredients in the front of the book for making coconut milk.

144

Quick Dobosh Torte

2 lb. pound cake
1 pkg. (6oz) choc. chips
1/4 C. boiling water
2 Tbs. confectioners sugar
4 egg yolks
1/4 lb. margarine
1 tsp. vanilla

Slice cake horizontally into 6 thin layers, chop up chocolate pieces in blender then add water & blend for 10 sec. Add remaining ingredients and blend for 30 seconds. Put icing in between every layer and cover cake.

Easier yet, buy low fat chocolate frosting already made, add about 1 Tbs. of water or Coconut Rum, or microwave about 30 sec. until soft enough to stir in rum... Make life easy on yourself. Decorate with fresh strawberries around edges with a line of whipped topping down the center. Makes an impressive dessert, Serves 6, but count on seconds!

'Dump Cake'

There are various recipes for this easy but delicious cake, so named because you dump everything into a baking dish.

1 21 oz can of blackberry, blueberry or cherry pie filling
1 8 oz can of crushed pineapple and juice
1/2 C melted butter
1/2 C coconut flakes
1 box white cake mix (French vanilla, extra moist is great)

Use a rectangular glass cake baking dish, 9" x 13", spray some oil spray on sides and bottom of dish. Evenly spread pie filling and pineapple on bottom, Spread the cake mix evenly, crushing any lumps. Pour the melted butter evenly over the top and sprinkle with coconut. Bake at 350* approximately 30 to 35 min. until lightly brown. After cooling, you may invert the cake, so the fruit is on top. This can get messy, so I recommend you keep it in the dish and spoon it out. A little whipped topping is great too!

Some other ideas; cherry pie filling, pineapple and chocolate cake mix. This has so many possibilities!

145

Easy Rocky Road Brownies

1 8.1 to 10.3 oz package brownie mix
1/4 C miniature marshmallows
1 C. walnuts, coarsely chopped
1/4 C semisweet chocolate pieces

Prepare as directed before cooking, sprinkle the above onto to uncooked mixture. Bake as directed....

Quick Black Forest Cake

1 box Devils Food cake mix
8 oz whipped topping
3 Tbs. coconut rum
1 12 oz. vanilla or chocolate instant pudding
1 can cherry pie filling

Mix cake according to directions, substituting 3 Tbs. water with the rum. Bake in a 9 x 13 in. cake pan. While cake is warm poke top with fork and spread cherry filling over cake. Prepare pudding. Fold whip topping into pudding, spread over pie filling. cover and refrigerate. Decorate, if desired, with 2 crushed "Heath" bars, or similiar candy bar, Whipped topping, pie filling cherries or whatever the mood strikes!

Raspberry Oatmeal Treats

1 pkg. white cake mix
2 C. quick cooking oats
3/4 C. margarine melted
1 12 oz. jar raspberry jam
1/2 C shredded coconut
1 Tbs. water

Combine mix, oats, coconut, and melted margarine until crumbly. Place 3 C. of dry mix in a 13" by 9 " pan and press down. Combine jam and water, spooning over crumb mix, spreading evenly. Cover with rest of mixture, patting firmly. Bake at 375* for 20 min. Cool and cut into bars. This is one of those perfect recipes for the kids to make!!

146

Quick Strawberry Torte

1 2 lb. pound cake
1 pkg. frozen strawberries
1 pint fresh strawberries
8 oz Cool Whip or whipped cream

Slice cake into 4 layers, Using half the fresh strawberries, mash and mix them with the defrosted strawberries. Add enough whipped cream so you can spread onto the cake layers. Frost sides and top with remaining whipped cream and decorate with the rest of the fresh strawberries. Makes a nice cool light dessert. Very impressive for company....

Orange Ice

My mom used to make this for me and it is the only frozen dessert I have in here, but it is for me, so I will always have it!

1 C sugar
1/2 C water
1 tsp. grated orange rind
1/4 C lime juice
2 C. orange juice
1/4 C water
1 tsp gelatin

Mix sugar, water and orange rind, boil 5 minutes. Cool. Allow gelatine to soak in 1/4 C water several minutes. Dissolve and add to sugar syrup with orange juice and lime juice. Pour into freezing tray and freeze to a firm mush. Remove to a chilled bowl and beat until light. Return to tray and finish freezing.

Pearla's Sweet Potato Pudding

8 C. grated raw sweet potato
6 C. coconut milk
2 C. brown sugar
1 C .evap. milk
3 Tbs. margarine
3/4 C. flour
1 tsp. nutmeg
1/2 tsp. cinnamon
1/2 Tbs. vanilla
2 Tbs. coconut rum (my addition)

Spray 13" x 9" pan with oil, and cook in a slow oven at 200* Start checking after one hour. Continue cooking, checking in 15 min. intervals and removing when cooked. It will take about 1 1/2 to 2 hours. Again an old time Cayman dessert, which I stray from the "native way" of eating by adding whipped topping! This recipe is from a lady friend of mine from West Bay!

Toffee Bar Cake

6 Heath bars, chopped into small pieces.
2 C. flour
2 C. brown sugar
1/2 C. margarine
1 t. baking soda
pinch of salt
1 egg
1 C. milk
1 tsp vanilla
1/2 C. pecans

Add chopped Heath bars, saving 1 cup for the top. Cream sugar and butter, add rest of ingredients. Pour into a 9 x 13 greased pan, sprinkle the rest of the Heath Bars over the top, and bake about 1/2 hr. at 350*.
Easy, and a delicious treat!

Easy Tiramisu

This Italian delight ismade with mascarpone, the classic Italian sweet cheese. However, it can be made with ricotta, which comes close to mascarpone with a touch of vanilla or almond flavoring.

light whipped topping
1/3 liquor; Kahlua or Tia Maria
1 lb. pound cake
1 C. ricotta cheese
1 tsp vanilla
1/2 C. sugar
1 C whipped topping
cocoa; about 1/8th C.
1 C coffee mix with 1/2 C coffee liquor

Beat together 1 C. ricotta cheese , vanilla, 1/2 C. powdered sugar. Fold in 1 C. whipped topping . Slice in 3 layers, long ways, and take the first layer of cake and place on serving plate, drizzle over 1/3rd of coffee mix, spread with 1/3rd of the cheese mixture, sprinkle on some cocoa powder, repeat with next layer and the top. Use whipped topping to cover entire exposed cake and decorate with some fresh strawberries on top and around the cake plate. The result is delicious, impressive and an attractive presentation. Serves 6 people.

Tiramisu

3 large eggs separated,   8 oz mascarpone cheese
1/2 C sugar   1/8th C. cocoa
1 C. strong coffee   20 lady fingers
2 Tbs cognac or brandy

Combine egg yolks, 1 Tbs. coffee, sugar, and cognac in large bowl, beat 3 to 4 min., add cheese, beat 3 to 5 min. until smooth. In another bowl beat egg whites with a little sugar until stiff, fold into yolk mixture. Pour rest of coffee mixture into a flat dish, dipping lady fingers one side and layering into a serving dish. Spread 1/3 of the cheese mixture and sprinkle with cocoa. Layer again repeating the first steps, finishing with the top cheese mixture layer. Refrigerate until ready to serve... Serves about 6 people

149

Christmas Pudding

A delicious old time Christmas Pudding. This recipe is from a wonderful, talented, accomplished and above all entertaining and interesting, friend of mine. Born in St Vincent, Lady Pamela Swaby, a English-Canadian, is a great cook and even greater character. Lucky you are if you should come across the opportunity to sit down and have a cup of coffee with Pam!

1 C. flour
1 tsp. soda
1 tsp. salt
1 tsp. cinnamon
1/4 tsp. nutmeg
3/4 tsp. mace

Mix in 3 C. raisins
3/4 lb citron
3/4 lb candied orange & lemon
2 C. walnuts chopped
1 1/2 C. soft bread crumbs

Mix in:
2 C. shortening
1 C. brown sugar
3 beaten eggs
1/3 C. currant jelly
1/4 C. fruit juice or brandy or sherry

Mix all in well greased 2 qt. mold
Steam 6 hours in oven (put in pan of water)

Hard Sauce

Cream until soft 1 C. margarine (1/2 lb)
2 C. sifted confectioners sugar
Beat in 1 unbeaten egg white. Stir in 1/2 tsp. vanilla.

Put in serving dish, sprinkle with nutmeg, and chill in refrigerator about an hour.

Guess who???
Dressed up as Sir Turtle in front of the Cracked Conch for a special promotion with the past CEO of Cayman Airways, Ray Wilson. I also wore this costume for the talent competition in the Glamorous Granny pageant!! I danced all over the stage to a song sang by Chuck and Barrie that was the Cayman Airways theme song. My family was up in the stands hootin' and hollering and cheering me on and laughing even harder.

Turtle Cake

1 chocolate cake mix
14 oz. caramels
1 C. chocolate chips
3/4 C. butter
1/2 evaporated milk
1 C. chopped nuts (walnuts or pecans)

Prepare cake mix according to directions, pour half into a 9 x 13 inch pan and bake at 350 for 15 min. Melt caramels, butter and milk on low heat stirring constantly. Pour over baked cake. Top with chocolate chips and nuts. Pour on rest of cake batter. Bake another 20 min. or until done. Delicious!
For best results when serving, make sure you put on a great costume like the one above to achieve maximum enjoyment for everyone involved!!

Someday

If I should ever be left all alone
And it gets really lonely in this big old home
I'll plan on a visit to my children and say
It's so good to be here--yes, I think I'll stay.
Then I'll live with my children and bring them great joy.
To repay all I've had from each girl and each boy
I shall draw on the walls and scuff up the floor;
Run in and out without closing the door.
I'll hide frogs in the pantry, socks under my bed.
Whenever they scold me, I'll hang my head.
I'll run and I'll romp, always fritter away
The time to be spent doing chores every day.
I'll pester my children when they're on the phone.
As long as they're busy I won't leave them alone.
Hide candy in closets, rocks in a drawer,
And never pick up my clothes from the floor.
Dash off to the movies and not wash a dish.
I'll plead for allowance whenever I wish.
I'll stuff up the plumbing and deluge the floor.
As soon as they've mopped it I'll flood it some more.
When they correct me, I'll lie down and cry,
Kicking and screaming, not a tear in my eye.
I'll take all their pencils and flashlights, and then
When they buy new ones, I'll take them again.
I'll spill glasses of milk to complete every meal,
Eat my banana and just drop the peel.
Put toys on the table, spill jam on the floor,
I'll break lots of dishes as though I were four.
What fun I shall have, what joy it will be to
Live with my children... the way they lived with me!

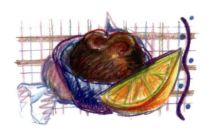

a bit o' candy

Debi's Candy

This is a candy Debi made for Christmas that was out of this world good!!

It is relatively easy;

peanut butter
confectioners sugar
condensed evaporated milk

white chocolate chips
heavy cream

Mix up the first three ingredients until you can roll into a ball. Then melt the white chocolate into a small amount of hot cream until mixture is the constancy to dip in the balls and not run off. Dip them in hot mixture and place on wax paper to cool. This is a problem because as everyone walks by they pick them up and eat them and there are very few left to put away!

Potato Candy
(an old Amish custom or is it Irish?)

Boil potatoes until able to mash, add confectioners sugar, (about 60% potato) if liquid is needed, no more than 1 Tbs. milk, knead. Roll about 2" pieces to look like miniature potatoes, roll them in a mixture of cinnamon and confectioners sugar, and they will look like a potato. Cool and eat!!! You can also add a little finely shredded coconut, these are really good!!

This is fun and easy for the kids on a bad day!! I met some an absolutely wonderful couple, Frank and Mary Jelinek from Pennsylvania and they were the only ones I ever met who knew what I was talking about!! However, they thought the origins were Irish? But then they are the real food experts with their own food show "Dining Around," on WWDB out of Philadelphia, Pennsylvania. They were a real inspiration! Guess where I found them.. "Dining around" at the Cracked Conch By the Sea, Grand Cayman!!

154

Divinity

This is an old and true way of using up egg whites, however, as the name indicates, it is really "divine". An old recipe using brown sugar is called "Sea Foam", and is equally delicious. This can be made by replacing the white sugar with brown sugar and 2 Tbs vinegar.

 4 C. sugar
 3/4 C. water
 1 C. light corn syrup
 4 egg whites
 1 Tbs. vanilla

Place egg whites in mixer bowl, to bring to room temperature before beating. Place syrup and water in pan and bring to a rolling boil, turn down slightly to avoid boiling over. Cover boiling for 3 minutes to dissolve sugar crystals. Uncover, continue boiling until the syrup comes to a "hard ball" stage. Have a glass of ice water and ice, drop into glass and wait until the ball of syrup turns into a hard ball when dropped and test by pulling out of water. Beat egg whites until they hold in stiff peaks, add, vanilla, then slowly pour the syrup into the egg whites. Nearing the end, you will increase the flow and mix rapidly. Beat mixture until you can drop on surface and it holds its shape. Do not panic when trying to reach this stage, keep beating, it will lose some gloss and it will start holding its shape. Butter or spray wax paper and proceed to drop candy on paper, using two spoons sprayed with shortening or butter. This may also be put into buttered pan and cut into squares when firm. Store in air tight container, when candy is firm or dried out.

Chopped nuts, coconut or crushed hard candy may be added for crunch. We like it just plain and smooth and "heavenly"!

Penuche

 2 C. brown sugar
 1 C white sugar
 1 cup evaporated milk
 2 Tbs. light corn syrup
 1 pinch salt
 2 Tbs. butter
 1 tsp vanilla

Stir over medium heat and cook until the soft ball stage, stirring frequently. Remove from heat and add butter. Let mixture cool down for about 1/2 hour then add vanilla and beat until creamy. You may then add your "crunch" and pour into greased 9" sq. buttered dish.

Nana goes to Washington!! She won a poetry competion for the poem 'Looking Beyond' which is in this book.

Jonee's Won't Fail Fudge

My mom's fudge is to die for! I always told her not to have sweets when I came to visit, so she would hide them in various covered tins, and invariably I would search and find them and eat them all!!!

>2/3 C. evaporated milk (1 small can)
>16 large marshmallows or a 7 oz jar fresh marshmallow cream
>1 1/3 C. sugar
>Pinch of salt
>1/4 C. margarine
>
>1 1/2 C. semi sweet chocolate. pieces
>1 tsp. real vanilla
>Optional: 1 C. chopped walnuts or pecans

Mix first 5 ingredients in heavy sauce pan. Stirring constantly, heat to boiling and boil 5 min. (candy thermometer 240* is soft boil). Remove from heat. Add choc. and stir till melted. Stir in vanilla, and nuts. Spread in buttered pan. Cool on rack till firm. Makes about 2 lbs.

Peanut Butter Fudge

A friend of my mom's, Marie Vail, who is a master 'goodies' cook gave us this delicious recipe.

2 C white sugar
2/3 C. evap. milk, boil together until soft ball stage or on candy
        thermometer. Remove from heat and add:
1 C. peanut butter (chunky peanut butter is delicious)
1 7 oz jar marshmallow cream

Pour into a buttered 8"x 8" pan, cut into squares when cool.

Coconut Fudge

My experimenting gave me this one. I love coconut. You just have to have it when you live in the Caribbean!!

1 C canned coconut cream
2 1/2C white sugar, boil together until the soft ball stage, (when it forms a soft ball in ice water). Remove from heat and add:
1 tsp vanilla
2 Tbs margarine or butter
1 C. grated coconut flakes..
1 7 oz jar of marshmallow cream

Stir until blended and spread into a buttered 7' x 11' rectangular pan or 8 x 8. Chill and try to resist!

Coconut Candy

You can always find this candy at gas stations and road side shops in sandwich bags. This is a real local recipe from a very special lady and great cook from West Bay. She said she does not want credit in case it does not turn out right! However, you really cannot go wrong.

2 dry coconuts, take out the meat and grate coconut (some like to cut in chunks but they are to hard to chew, some grind it in the blender but that is too fine.)
4 C water
4 C sugar (white sugar; to which you can add food coloring if you like or brown sugar, which I prefer. I think it gives a better flavor)

Boil them together until they are sticky. Place on wax paper and if they are gummy add more sugar and boil a bit more.
You can always use a glass of ice water and make sure they reach the hard ball stage.

If you want to add fresh grated ginger, which many people do, you may add it to the brown sugar version. Otherwise, I like it just plain without the "stingy" ginger!

Anyway, enjoy our 'local candy'!

a subject very close to my heart: DIETS

Dieting

What follows is a collection of what I've found to be tried and true short term diets. No book on food written by yours truly could ever be complete without some sort of tribute to dieting. In my love affair with food, I've often found it necessary to take off a few pounds here and there and I've always been open to a quick fix. I feel with dieting, you can be as creative as with cooking!

These have been referred to as 'fad diets'. As per the usual, you need to check with your doctor first. As I have always been vain about my weight, I have accumulated many diet plans and have singled our a few that have worked for me in the short term. Diets, spaced sensibly over time, have helped me maintain a healthy weight even with the way I love to cook and eat, finding immense pleasure in the taste and textures of the food. I also have a love for chocolate, pecan pie, eggs Benedict, and just about everything else in this cook book!

A diet known as the low carbohydrate Air Force diet was widely gaining attention in the 60's and back then it was also called 'The Drinking Man's Diet' allowing certain types of alcoholic beverages. Another similar one was called the low carbohydrate Air Force diet, not eliminating carbohydrates but controlling them. I am getting ahead of myself as the real first experiments with eliminating carbohydrates and sugar go back to Dr. William Harvey and a London coffin-maker, William Banting, who was about five and a half feet tall and over 200 lbs. In 1864, he wrote and published, 'A Letter on Corpulence' telling of his miraculous loss of weight; he could now bend over and tie his shoelaces among other things. His weight had previously prevented him from doing many day-to-day tasks.

Some years ago around 1946, an experimental diet was introduced to a handful of executives of the E. I. Dupont Company in Wilmington, Delaware. They were put on a diet of protein and fat under the direction of Dr. Albert W. Pennington and Dr. George H. Gehrmann. My Father was one of these candidates and was very happy on the diet. He lost weight by eating things he loved. He also found the 'Mayo Clinic Diet' (I understand they were really never associated with it) was also successful and I will give it to you as well.

The high protein diets were in fashion again in the 70's and 80's. Then it was low carbohydrates, then liquid diets, and today the high protein diet is back. The Atkins Diet has made a great comeback with people really losing weight and maintaining it with Dr. Atkins maintenance instructions. I had the pleasure of meeting the late Dr. Atkins and am convinced he has contributed greatly to the diet industry.

After experiencing a heart problem and being "saved" by the cardiologists at the Miami Heart Institute, I recommend the South Beach Diet. It is written by Dr. Arthur Agatston, a famous cardiologist who is with Mt. Sinai Medical Center, which is affiliated with the Miami Heart Institute.

I strongly feel the way of the future is to see a Doctor and a Nutritionist to obtain an evaluation of our system's metabolism, our blood levels and what nutrients we are lacking, and also any health problems which need to be taken into consideration. In this way we will really learn about our own individual needs and know just what foods we need to and which to avoid in order to maintain our healthiest balance.

We have all heard enough of how we should eat right, stay away from fats, sweets and desserts. True, pick up a piece of fruit instead of that chocolate cake or candy. Beware of sugar and read those labels; the sugar content in a glass of juice or soda can be equal to a total days limit. So for that lifelong healthy regimen, just eat right.

However, when you get down on yourself and depression sets in over your weight, which happens to a lot of us, there are some very good quick remedies that will knock off some pounds and make you feel better. Again you should check with your Doctor... I have printed the "claims" and the diet as they have been given to me and some of the loss of pounds seem to be high. I had removed this chapter previously, but I still get calls for some of these diets and felt having them to refer to would be beneficial. Someone called it the "underground diet faxes"!

Following are copies of some of these 'fad diets':

The Mayo Clinic Diet

The 3 Day Diet

The Miracle Soup Diet

Mayo Clinic Diet #1
(This was from about 1950's)

Breakfast
>   1/2 grapefruit or unsweetened juice
>   2 eggs any style
>   2 slices bacon (minimum)
>   1 C plain coffee or tea
>   (You may eat 12 eggs and 12 slices of bacon if you wish)

Lunch
>   1/2 Grapefruit
>   Meat any style amount, with gravy providing it is not thickened with flour
>   Salad any amount with dressing that has no sugar

Dinner
>   1/2 Grapefruit
>   Meat any style
>   Vegetable green, yellow, or red
>   Salad any amount with dressing that has no sugar

Snack
>   Tomato Juice or skim milk

1. At each meal you must eat until you are full, until you cannot possibly eat any more.
2. Don't eliminate anything - it is the combination of foods that burns up accumulated fat.
3. The grapefruit is important because it acts as a catalyst that starts the fat-burning process.
4. Cut down on coffee, it is thought to affect the insulin balance that hinders the burning-up process. Try to limit yourself to 1 C per meal.
5. No eating between meals. If you eat the combination of food suggested until you are stuffed, you won't be hungry between meals.
6. Note that this diet completely eliminated sugar and starches which form lipids, and lipids form fat. Fat helps to burn fat so you can fry your eggs in butter and use butter generously on vegetables.
7. Eat until you are full then force yourself to eat more. The more you eat of the proper combination of food, the more you will lose.
8. You can lose 10 lbs in 10 days, There will be no weight loss the first four days, but you will suddenly drop 5 lbs on the 5th day.
9. Then you will lose 1 lb each day until the 10th day. Then you will lose 1/2 lb to 1 1/2 lbs every 2 days until you get down to your proper weight.
10. This is not a caloric diet, but a clinical diet, that is why it is important you eat everything with no substitutions.

Editors note: To me the 12 eggs and 12 slices of bacon seem bit much... However, people that went on it had success. Again this follows the basic principles of the Atkins Diet.

162

Mayo Clinic Diet #2

This is the one my father followed that was very successful. It isn't painful, and does work, I have done it also. You can see similiarities between the diets but this does give you some carbohydrates. Lose up to 20 lbs in 14 Days.

1. No substitutes whatsoever.
2. No alcoholic beverages.
3. Do not stay on diet for more than 14 days
4. Abstain from everything not included here.
5. One must eat exactly as assigned below.
6. No eating between meals except raw celery and raw carrots.
7. Prepare salads without oil or mayonnaise. Use lemons and vinegar.
8. All vegetables are to be eaten without butter.
9. Lean Meat only.
10. Coffee black, tea plain,; you can use a non caloric sweetener.
11. It is not necessary to eat everything but do not substitute or add. Diet maintains normal energy while reducing. Quantities are less important, but indicated combinations should be observed.

Breakfast: The same everyday: Grapefruit, 1 slice of bread toasted, coffee or tea

Monday	Lunch: cold cuts of lean meat and tomatoes Dinner: Fish, combination salad (as many vegetables as you wish), 1 piece dry toast, grapefruit.
Tuesday	Lunch: Fruit salad (as much as you want, any kind) Dinner: Plenty of steak, tomatoes, lettuce, celery, olives, Brussel sprouts or cucumbers.
Wednesday	Lunch: Tuna fish, or salmon, salad, with lemon, grapefruit. Dinner: Two lamb chops or chicken, celery, cucumbers, tomatoes.
Thursday	Lunch: Cold turkey, spinach Dinner: Two eggs, cottage cheese, cabbage 1 piece of dry toast.
Friday	Lunch: Assorted cheese slices, spinach, 1 piece of dry toast. Dinner: Fish, combination salad (as many vegetables as you wish), 1 piece of dry toast.
Saturday	Lunch: Fruit salad (as much as you want, any kind) Dinner: Cold chicken, tomatoes, grapefruit.
Sunday	Lunch: Chicken, tomatoes, carrots, cooked cabbage, broccoli or cauliflower, grapefruit Dinner: Plenty of steak, celery, cucumbers or Brussel sprouts, tomatoes

Miracle Soup

Cut vegetables in medium pieces and cover them with water. Cook high for 10 minutes, turn down soup and simmer until cooked. Eat as much as you want, in the frequency that you want, any time of the day. The more you eat, the more weight you lose.

Soup

3 white onions, 1/2 head of cabbage, 1 bunch of scallions, 1 28 oz. can diced tomatoes, 2 green bell peppers, 1 head of celery, 1 large can V-8 juice , 1 packs dry onion soup, 1 -2 bouillon cubes, if desired.

Chop vegetables, combine all ingredients in a large stock pot, add enough water to cover. Boil for 10 minutes. Reduce to a simmer and continue cooking until vegetables are tender. Eat as much as you want, whenever you want, at any time of the day. You may leave half of it with the chopped vegetables and put the rest in a blender. I find the blended one when it is really chilled is refreshing and delicious. Like drinking a super vitamin V8 juice. Also it is good to put a cup in the microwave and heat up, giving you a pick me up hot drink!

Diet Hints:
Drink at least 8 glasses of water per day, coffee and tea only using artificial sweetener. Diet sodas are fine, however there is conflicting opinions, as to their effect on your weight with some factions believing they actually cause a chemical reaction to keep weight on. So take water instead.

If you follow this 7 day diet you could loose up to 10 lbs per week.

The efficiency of this 7 day diet is that the consumed food burns more calories than it adds to your body in caloric value. This plan is full of healthy foods and If followed properly, it will cleanse your system of impurities and give you a sensation of fullness. It will give you energy and you should feel lighter.

1st. Day: Any fruit except bananas, plus soup and water. Eat all the fruits that you can possibly eat. Melon lovers, this is your day. Drink unsweetened tea and cranberry juice and plenty of water. You could loose 3 lbs.

2nd Day: Vegetables, all the fresh veggies raw or cooked, including potatoes, soup and water. Try to eat green leaves (spinach, lettuce, etc.) and stay far from beans, peas, and corn. For a real treat you may eat a baked potato with butter.

164

3rd. Day: Fruit and Vegetables (same as 1st and 2nd day), except no potatoes. Eat plenty of soup and drink your water.

4th Day: Bananas and Skim milk to a maximum of 8 bananas and 8 glasses of skim milk, maintaining the same amount. This will supply the much needed proteins, potassium, and carbohydrates, plus the soup and water.

5th Day: Meat and Tomatoes, up to 10 to 20 ounces of beef, chicken or fish and up to 6 tomatoes, plus soup and water, distributed throughout the day. Hit the water hard to help eliminate the uric acid from your body. Make certain you have your soup at least once.

6th Day: Meat, chicken or fish (any kind) and vegetable (all that you want, except potatoes), plus soup, leafy greens, and water.

7th Day: Natural brown rice, unsweetened fruit juices and lots of vegetables, plus soup and water.

This particular diet has supposedly come from Spain and the original is unknown. No alcoholic beverages are allowed. If you become constipated you may eat a cup of bran. You may have black coffee.

Do not cheat! No fried foods, no bread, no carbonated beverages; not even diet soda. On your meat days you may substitute steak with broiled, poached, or baked skinless chicken and fish, and seasoning with some of your blended soup makes a tasty treat.

The very best way to do this diet is to have a buddy to do it with. My friend Angela and I went to Cayman Brac, stayed in a lovely cottage and just tended to ourselves. She called it a women's 'time out'! Our only decisions were to have the soup hot, cold, ground up or chopped!! On the day of the banana, we made shakes adding vanilla, artificial sweetener, and ice and put it in a blender. We thought we had died and gone to heaven! I had trouble with the brown rice, but again the soup mixture can be cooked with the rice, making it a bit more palatable.

Three Day Diet

(supposedly lose 10 lbs in 3 days)
This also came with the heading "The Canadian Heart Foundation Three Day Diet". I find this to be a bearable diet break.

Breakfast: Black Coffee or Tea

Day 1
   Breakfast: 1/2 Grapefruit, 1 slice toast and 2 Tbs peanut butter
   Lunch: 1/2 C tuna, 1 slice toast, coffee or tea.
   Dinner: 2 slices any type of meat (about 3 oz.) chicken, roast, etc.
   1 C. string beans, 1 C beets, 1 small apple, 1 C vanilla ice cream, coffee
   or tea.

Day 2
   Breakfast: 1 egg, 1 slice toast, 1/2 banana
   Lunch: 1 C cottage cheese, 5 saltine crackers.
   Dinner: 2 Hot Dogs (no bun), 1 C broccoli, 1/2 C carrots, 1/2 banana, 1/2
   C vanilla ice cream.

Day 3
   Breakfast: Saltine crackers, 1 slice cheddar cheese, 1 small apple.
   Lunch:1 Hard boiled egg, 1 slice toast.
   Dinner: 1 C tuna or any fish, 1 C beets, 1 C cauliflower, 1/2 Cantaloupe,
   1/2 C vanilla ice cream.

Note: this diet works on chemical breakdown and is proven. Do not vary or substitute any of the above foods. Salt & pepper may be used. But no other seasonings. Where no quantity is given, there are no restrictions other than common sense. This diet is to be used 3 days at a time.

In 3 days you can lose up to 10 lbs. After 3 days of dieting, you can eat your normal foods, but do not overdo it. After your 4 days of normal eating, start back on the 3 day diet. You can lose up to 40 lbs in a month, if you stick to this diet. It is a safe diet. Remember: Do not "pick" in between meals.

Bob and I on a Florida fishing trip with Jim, kris, Karie and Harrison.
I suppose you can guess what we had for dinner that night.

The Ultimate Fitness Way to Eat

My retirement began with taking my husband in hand and heading to the best choice I could make for a fitness and longevity center. As luck would have it, after much research, I chose the Pritikin Longevity Center in Aventura, Florida. What an eye opening experience. We stayed for the recommended two weeks.

We learned so much about nutrition from the resident nutritionist, doctors, weight clinics, cooking classes and lectures.

I would recommend any of the books on the New Pritikin Program, by Robert Pritikin, son and assistant researcher to Nathan Pritikin. Their clinical research for diabetes and heart disease has proven that the Pritikin diet and exercise program works. Always interested in diet and nutrition, I bought my first book in 1990. Reading it made sense. At one point I said I never would weigh myself again. That is the biggest mistake of my life. Anyway, I now weigh in every morning! Our weight is coming off slowly, but we feel right about it!

As we checked into the center, blood was taken and a complete work up was done. We were given a physical, tested, and our two week exercise program was designed. We were told the maximum heart rate we needed to reach every day in cardio class, which was carefully monitored. We had 4 hours of exercise a day, lots of lectures and classes and the meals were monitored. No caffeine, sugar, salt, oil, white flour, no white pasta, no egg yolks, only no fat dairy, bison once per week, a small amount of chicken, a little seafood! They have Ezekiel Bread, a whole grain bread with no flour, which is also made in raisin.

Believe me, once you have that as toast, you are hooked! That is at least one thing we were doing right! Basically you are going through a detox of the poisons in your body!! You can treat yourself to a lot of spa services and with all the exercising, a massage is wonderful and necessary!

Our blood was taken and checked 3 times in 2 weeks. Everyone's numbers fall!! Vitamin intake is recommended, and the amount of calories per day is recommended. You are pulled through the first week of getting to 1 hour of cardio per day, weights every other day for 1/2 hour, and the importance of stretching about 45 min. per day. Optional is water aerobics daily, yoga, band stretching, etc. It's good because you're with a lot of people in the same boat, trying, not giving up, and working very hard to meet goals for healthier living. There is food all day long; you are encouraged to eat 6 times per day. Plenty of soup, fruits, vegetables, and salads, dressings without oil. You can eat whenever and however much you want to eat. They are recommending 49% of your food should be from fiber. They recommend Splenda for your sweetener. Since leaving the center we have discovered new ways to add taste to our food. Walden Farms makes some fabulous sugar and fat free dressings.

All in all the experience was very good. We're not going to become vegetarians, as are many of the professional staff at the center. Trying to eat healthy, our fridge has a lot more fruit; we are never without a variety of delicious berries. We still try to eat our oatmeal for breakfast, maybe decaf coffee, perhaps a slice of Ezekiel toast with no fat cream cheese, 2 cups of salad before lunch, plenty of soup. Decaf tea is highly recommended and we do drink more tea. This experience has been the ultimate in living well and being healthy. We hope you will also look into it.

family recipes

Recipes for the family; for the heart, the mind, and the soul.

The "kitchen" used to be the heart of our homes, with all the family gathered around anticipating the good things produced by family members. It seems that our modern day society with everyone running, working, dieting, and attending meetings, we may have gotten away from the pleasures in the kitchen and sitting down together to share the day's activities and a good meal. That was how it used to be, sometimes it still is, but if it is a missing ingredient in your home, I am hoping some of these special 'family recipes" will bring a smile and perhaps stimulate some good "old fashioned fun centered around the kitchen...

The first part might help with being a parent, sharing tips and ideas that might just work. The next step, of course, is being a grandparent, and last, a role many of us never planned to step into, being a stepparent. The rest is in support of the ideas, suggestions, and ideals from the lighter side in poems and sayings. Some humorous aging antidotes are also included. These are words our family has shared and enjoyed, and we hope you will too....

Raising children is a challenge in any day and age. After years in this field, raising five children, having three stepchildren, and presently nineteen grandchildren, I wish to impart some good hard-learned practical suggestions:

Parents...

So you are going to be "parents", a most exciting time!! Be loving and firm, use your common sense and trust in your instincts. Sometimes you can read too many books on child rearing. Books written by child experts can sometimes send out mixed messages. I know one such expert that supported "permissiveness" so as not to hinder the child's personality. Some of those children created a generation of rude, mannerless, and emotionally unbalanced, people, leaving them behind in dealing with society. This expert in his later years claimed he was "misunderstood".

Communicate.. find interesting ways to communicate. Hold family meetings, with everyone giving input of some kind or other. Make each member feel a part of the big picture. Each child is an individual and needs a different set of tender tools to assist in the

170

painful process of growing up. Know your child, his personality, his sensitivity, give encouragement and praise and always be sincere. Children know when you are dishonest. When they reach a stage of getting into everything, distract them by giving them their toy or something they can play with and teach them there

being positive, it is a lighter load. Have a sense of humor. If you do not you will be lost!!! Teach them it is OK to be silly and you try it too! I always find Halloween a perfect time to exercise that tool!

Mealtime...

This is a serious problem in some homes. Occasionally, one spouse

plenty of positive things to discuss, make it interesting and try to learn each other's goals and daily accomplishments. Do be careful that the children do not take over, but are involved in the conversation with respect for their elders and their manners.

To me, these ingredients are the most important recipes I can share, and they really are tried and true.

are things that belong to mommies and daddies and are off limits to them. Do not make wimps out of your kids. If they fall, don't make a big thing of it, but be there to help and support if they are hurt. Throw away negativism... it is a bad habit some people wake up with and drag around all day... It is a burden. Pick up on

chooses to quarrel with the other one or pick on a child or discuss a bad report card, etc.

This is a serious detriment to a happy family and can lead to other physical problems. It becomes hard to digest food, even great food when someone is wrangling over anything and everything. There are

Young children need to develop good eating habits. This "modern day" phenomenon of I don't eat that, "I don't like that", complain, complain, complain, seems to have gotten out of hand. Children should learn at an early age that it is a privilege to sit at the table with their family and eat what is put in front of them. Encourage them to eat a balanced diet and teach them which foods do what for their growing body and which foods have no food value, but actually can harm the body, even though they taste good....

Mom and Dad, decide how you want to bring up

your children.. If you disagree on something, do it in private, not in front of the children as it causes confusion and encourages them to play one parent against the other. That is definitely not good, leading to early lessons of manipulation. Share with them your faith, heeding the old saying, "families that pray together, stay together". Be able to listen to your children, encourage them to form their own opinion on all kinds of things and help them to think for themselves. Let them know they can come and tell you anything... even if they feel it is terrible. Keep your cool, their trust, and confidence that you will not turn on them if they trust in you... Many times I had to say a prayer to keep me calm, when they told me something shocking, so we could "deal with the problem together"; but it can be hard to keep "cool" about it.

Television

The television and computer...times and programs need to be regulated according to your lifestyles. I used to tell my kids, "don't just sit there and vegetate in front of a TV!!" Parents are so busy these days working, that to come home and go for a walk with your kids sounds exhausting, but if you do it you will feel better!!! Sit down together and play family games. Try charades, that is a real eye opener! Play sports together; taking in fresh air and exercise will set foundations for life-long positive habits and good health.

Home Rules

Young children need to be taught the home rules and their responsibilities to the family. They need to know the guidelines and that their negative actions will have "consequences"... Like truth or consequences........ Children are smarter than we sometimes give them credit for, and parents who set the consequences for say not doing homework and lying about it, should know the outcome will be no TV for the next 3 days or another of their favorite things to do being withdrawn. . A favorite pastime or toy taken away and can be earned back by good behavior.

Honesty

Be honest with your children. When they ask you a question, never lie, be honest . You are laying building blocks for their future and deceit is not included in a firm foundation. These foundations start from the beginning; if you try to start them from 3 years old you are too late; it must be done from the infant stage. An infant knows your tone of voice and builds love and trust from your caring. On the other hand an infant can distinguish nervousness, a lack of caring and love, resulting in a fussy baby.

Material Things

Teach them to deal with stress and peer pressure, to sift out the really important things in life and not the material things that some children seem to flaunt about, making others seem left out. Teach them that cruelty and meanness to others is unacceptable behavior, give them a sense of thankfulness for the blessings they have, and show them that envy and want are negative feelings that will only cause them to be unhappy.

Independence

Give them lots of love, channel their energy to good things, and make sure they know they are "special" and different from any other person in the world! Don't spoil them. Beware that you do not over protect them. To do so is denying them their learning experiences, if you run after them each time they take a little spill, encourage them to get up and go for it again... Know the times to let them go.. Probably the hardest thing to do. You need to practice this all along the way. Encourage them to be on their own and to be independent. I see Mothers who think they are doing a wonderful job by creating "clingy" children, when all they are doing is satisfying their own insecurity and denying their child normal and necessary growth experiences.

Grandparenting

Now this is a whole different ball game, for not only do you have the grandchildren to juggle but you have to be very careful not to step on the new parents' "territory"...... If you know what I mean. When they get two or three children, they ease up a bit, but with that first one, bite your lip, hold your advice, and monitor your "helpful suggestions." Forget about really spoiling them, follow your same consistent rules and help your kids out so that when the children visit you and go home they are not monsters. We find the Grandchildren are sometimes easier to handle (our way) without the parents. Many times the children will act up with Mom and Dad around, and it is difficult for you to enforce your rules. Make your rules clear and they will usually respect them. In our home, we have our grandkids' "place", where they can go and open the cabinet door, go to their

shelf and pull out the box with "their toys, coloring stuff, etc." Before they leave they must put everything away. It is interesting how the babies catch on at an early age and become quite proud of their ability to be like the big kids!! Another fun thing we do is to have

Make your family gatherings fun, creative and unforgettable. Here's our happy group at a Mary Kay party, husbands, babies and all.

them pick partners, usually an older child with the younger one, to hold hands, walk together, and help each other when we go places. We have such fun with our grandchildren, always trying to dream up adventures... cave hunting, kayaking, boating, snorkeling, going to the park. We enjoy it more if our children join us on those outings. Kids love to help in the kitchen, as long as it is done in a "fun" way. We spend time in there with them, as the photos reveal!

Support your own kids as best you can, be there when they need you. Try to be there for the birth of their child, as it is a very important event in your child's life and something that you should want to share with them. Always remember the grandkids are their children and they want to have the right to raise them "their way", which usually is not too far off from how they were raised!

Oh no...

I must share a funny story of one of my misadventures with my daughter's first daughter... She was working and not feeling too well, so in my anxiousness to help out, I decided to trim my granddaughter's hair, which I had done for my other daughter's daughter... without adverse results. So I trimmed the hair even... and what did I do that for? I thought the parents would never speak to me again!! I had overstepped my bounds, should have asked, etc. etc. I finally told the children that with so many grandkids, I needed a rule book for each family as I was getting mixed up as to what I could do with whom, when, and how!!!

Stepparenting

Perhaps this is the most difficult of all! We have joined together 8 children, their spouses and now the grandchildren that have come along. It was tough, but well worth it, especially when we all celebrate holidays together. Whatever the reasons for becoming a stepparent, it is a serious and tender spot to be in, however one that many people share these days.

This is a time when honesty, respect, and dignity need to guide your actions. When you marry someone with children, you become a stepparent. You cannot replace the Mother or Father, so keep your emotions and respect for the real parent in proper perspective and never let them feel threatened that you are trying to take over their child. Be there in a supportive role, deal with over active emotions with kindness and reason. Communicate your concerns, but do so with love. We have always tried to treat everyone the same, yet complying with their unique needs and differences.

A "Stepmother" once told me, there was no reason to get all the children together, as they were from different families. Her children visited the couples new home and his own children were made to feel unwelcome. One couple had no water in their home and when they asked if they could bathe in their fathers house, were told by the "stepmother", they could do so in the outside rinse off shower by the pool... come on! In the beginning of your new relationship together, life long hurts can be created by one spouse or the other toward the stepchildren. This, my friend can start a long rocky road in your marriage as well as unnecessary "heart hurts".

One of our greatest pleasures, when we take the grandkids out and tell them to choose up partners, is that they usually choose one of the "other side" of the

Bob and daughter-in-law Sherlyn with a bunch of the grandkids about to explore the North Side caves. Note the little ones--they really love a big kid adventure!

Grandparenting is a privilege. As my husband says, "If he had known grandchildren were so much fun, he would have had them first!"

family.... It takes patience, and understanding and sometimes you will be hurt, but hold up your head and move forward with a positive and caring attitude.

Family Gatherings

Wonderful times, holidays, birthdays, etc. are the perfect time for a family gathering. Our family started with the babies, then the smaller children, we would feed them first so the adults could sit down and eat with some semblance of sanity. As the children got a little older, they would still eat first, then go to one of the rooms, to plan and practice a "show" for us when we were all done eating and the majority of the clean up was done. This proved to be so much fun, we really look forward to it. Some of the children that are shy are given the opportunity to shine, and they do. Other times we will have everyone participate by standing up in front of us all and saying "What family means to them". Or Christmas, Thanksgiving or what every occasion you choose. Sometimes we ask them to write a poem before they come and read it at the appropriate time.

Also since our family has grown so, everyone brings something to eat, which has eased the work on just one person. I also feel it is rewarding to have the family prayer circle, holding hands, with each one saying a small prayer. All of these ideas can be worked out to suit your family, but they are important to bind the family. You will be amazed at the "heartfelt" things that can happen, making the family gathering something to treasure!

Don't ever miss a chance for a good hug and kiss! Here we are in our beautiful Frank Sound house which Bob built by himself.

At a recent family gathering, one of our youngest Granddaughters, Melanie, age 7 at the time, unbeknownst to anyone, brought this poem and stood up to read it for us all;

A Family

A family is a blessing;
it means so many things
Words could never really tell the joy a family brings...
A family is mutual love.
The love of a dad and mother—
Showing children how to love and care for one another...
A family is heartfelt pride, the feeling deep and strong,
That makes us glad to play a part
and know that we belong...
A family is always home,
a place where we can share
our joys and sorrows, hopes and dreams,
For happiness lives there...
A family is a bond of faith that even time can't sever,
A gift to last throughout our lives—

A family is forever!!

Here's Bob getting ready to take off on a motorcycle adventure with grandson Zak as concerned mom Barrie looks on.

Grandchildren

Today I took my grandchild, her little hand in mine,
I marveled at God's miracles and this child so fine.
I do not give them candy, nor expensive material things,
I take them to the little bird, to hear how sweet she sings,

I hope they say "My Omi loved me so, you see,
Because she took the time to do good things with me.
She took us in the car and when we got too loud,
She had us sing, now we can sing before a crowd!"

She told us a special gift from God goes out to everyone,
To learn to use it everyday, and when the day is done
Thank God for all the blessings he has bestowed upon us all,
To always keep God in our hearts, to keep us from a fall.

Thank you for these miracles, of grandchildren so fine,
Thank you for all of them, with their little hands in mine.

To be a Giver

It's not the things that can be bought that are life's richest treasure,
It's just the little "heart gifts" that money cannot measure..
A cheerful smile, a friendly word, a sympathetic nod,
Are priceless little treasures from the storehouse of our God.
They are the things that can't be bought with silver or with gold,
For thoughtfulness and kindness and love are never sold
They are the priceless things in life for which no one can pay,
And the giver finds rich recompense in giving them away.

Old Tyme Cures

Sometimes survival on a tiny island depends on how industrious you are and what you're willing to try in order to get better when you're ill! The advice and occasionally strange old-time cures are plenty in these parts and printed here for your enjoyment...

Mustard Plaster

Well now, this is definitely not to eat!! However, no cookbook should be complete without it. This one sticks with me forever as the most horrific cure for a chest cold that was ever used in days gone by. It has the most awful odor and if any "cure" worked in the past, this was surely it! In desperation I tried it on my poor ailing husband and it did work. However, I made it too strong because after having used old tinned mustard that was dead and thus not effective in my first attempt, I got my hot little hands on some fresh mustard. I put it on his chest and left it on too long which I soon found causes a burn.... Can you believe it?

My husband knows this now and try as I may, I'll never be able to get near him with it again! Actually, when I was in nurse's training years ago, they still gave out this recipe.

3 Tbs flour
1 Tbs. fresh tinned mustard,
water to mix

After working into a plaster, spread on wax paper and cover with another sheet of wax paper. Place cheesecloth next to chest, cover nipples with Vaseline and extra pieces of gauze and place prepared plaster on chest. This gets hot and hotter so make sure you do not burn the patient. Just cook the ribs till done, so to speak, until the cough loosens up. This may or may not happen, as the patient will shortly become so miserable that he instantly feels better and claims the cold is gone. At any rate, a miraculous recovery!

Caster Bean Plant Leaf Herbal Wrap

To break a fever, fetch plenty of caster bean plant leaves, heat them over used kerosene in an old fashioned lamp and then wrap the patient in them. Here, here, this works well. Years ago, when we were out on the end of the island and there was no doctor, my little daughter, Sheree, had a terrible fever. I tried everything from the medical world to bring the fever down. The fever hit 103 degrees and my baby was so sick. At this point I was willing to try almost anything. I used this and sure enough, the fever broke soon after the total body wrap. I do believe in these herbal remedies and have witnessed many amazing cures!

"Cerce" Tea

I know a boy named Percy
Whose Mother gave him "Cerce"
And he bawled, "Lord have Mercy!"

This is a tea made of the "Cerce" vine. It is thought to cleanse the blood. It is bitter, pity, I used to tell my kids and then make them drink it.

I drank it too, and still do when I can get some. It tastes so bad it has to be good for you.

Cider Vinegar and Honey Libation

Capt. Frank Roulstone used to drink cider vinegar and honey every afternoon and claimed it cured everything. He was always skinny, so maybe it even kept him thin. After much consideration, I figure that this is similar to the new theory about red wine preventing plaque from forming in the arteries. Frank's drink and red wine have similar ingredients. Stranger things have happened!

Aloe Vera

A healing plant, aloe vera is one of the most widely used substances around for medicine and beauty products and it grows right here in everybody's back yard. Aloe has long been the "secret ingredient" for fixing burns, wrinkles, and minor skin injuries. People drink it by cutting off about 2" of the leaf, peeling it and putting it in the blender with cranberry juice, apple juice and left over fruits, like banana, grapes, apple, mango, etc. Just break one of the thick pointed spiky leaves to get the clear gel-like sap and you have your miracle cure. Great for sunburns! Refer to my ingredients chapter in the beginning of the book.

Cure for Gangrene

I did not get the recipe for this, but the story was so incredible I have to share it with you. In 1963, a man was working as a gardener for the Merren family at Pageant Beach Hotel. He was cutting the yard, when a piece of rock flew and hit him in the leg. He went to the hospital after it became infected and they dressed it with the normal medications and told him to return to work. He did and it only got worse. The wound eventually became gangrenous. The hospital said they could only recommend he have it amputated as soon as possible as they saw little hope for improvement. His wife got in touch with Lingard McLaughlin, his father-in-law. He made a native poultice, which my husband carried down to the man. He had put it on our bedspread and it tipped over and stained the yellow bedspread a horrible black-brown color that smelled terrible. He took the poultice to the man and he applied it to the leg that evening. The next day he returned to the hospital and the gangrene had not spread and the color was returning to the gangrenous area. By the day after, the infection was gone, the leg was saved, and I saw it all with my own eyes. Let me tell you, I sure believe in the native cures! Who knows what was in the mysterious smelling concoction...